Week 45

Eat, Sleep and Walk:
Stories From The Camino

by Len "P.D." MacDonald

I would like to give special thanks to my daughter, Ellie MacDonald, who edited this book.

Thanks to Jean Pearcey of Jeanious Designs for designing the book cover.

I would like to thank Clare Lazzuri for assisting with some of the technical aspects of the book, getting an ISBN number, and arranging a copyright for the book.

Thanks to Justin Gregg, who assisted me once again in the printing process.

Canadian Cataloguing in Publication Data

MacDonald, Leonard, 1951-

Eat, Sleep and Walk: Stories From The Camino

ISBN 978-0-9920706-4-9

1161714©2019

Website: www.week45.com

Preface

The Camino de Santiago, known as The Way of St. James, is a network of pilgrims' ways or pilgrimages leading to the shrine of the apostle St. James The Great in the cathedral of Santiago de Compostela (Santiago) in northwest Spain. Located in Galicia, tradition has it that the remains of the saint are buried here. The Way of St. James was one of the most important Christian pilgrimages of the latter Middle Ages. Many walkers, or pilgrims, follow its routes today as a spiritual journey. It is also very popular with hikers and cyclists.

Several years ago, before I retired, I met a friend while walking to work one morning. He had just returned from walking the Camino, with which I was unfamiliar at the time, and began to tell me about his experience. I had become an avid walker since having retired from running marathons and the seeds were sown that day for a vision of my own journey across Spain.

My desire was further cemented when a family member walked the Camino in 2018 and, upon their return, I was mesmerized by their description of the walk. I decided then and there that this was something I had to do.

In May of 2019 I flew to Spain, took a train from Madrid to Pamplona and began my Camino adventure.

This book is an account of my daily walks. It contains some historical information and also a description of what I felt and experienced for twenty-five days and 713 kilometres. Mostly, the book is about the wonderful people from all over the world that I met along the way. I interviewed more than 30 of them and their stories appear in each chapter of the book.

Lace up your shoes, readers, and come for a walk with me!

Index

Chapter 1 – Pamplona to Cirauqui

31k/46,193 Steps

The first leg of my journey took me from Pamplona to the town of Cirauqui. The high point of this stage (literally and figuratively) is Alto del Perdón. There are some impressive wind turbines in this area but the most memorable landmark here is the wrought iron representation of pilgrims. Descending this mountain is very tricky, with a lot of large, loose stones. One of the major towns on this route is Puente La Reina (The Queen's Bridge), where a Romanesque bridge spans the Arga River. Approximately eight kilometres further lies Cirauqui, my first stop on the Camino. It is a fairly steep climb to get into town and an even steeper climb up to the albergue.

Albergues, or hostels, are a fixture on the Camino. There are two types of albergues: the "official" albergue is usually owned and run by the local government for the area, often referred to as Municipals. The cost is in the range of five to seven Euros per night. These places provide a bed, a blanket (most of the time!), washroom facilities and a place to wash clothes by hand. Room sizes vary but this is communal living, complete with rows of bunkbeds. If you are a light sleeper this may not be your best option, as you could find yourself in a small room with two bunkbeds or a large dorm with 50. Snoring is the unofficial soundtrack of albergue, but after several long days of walking a person becomes acclimatised and is normally so tired that sleep eventually comes. Sometimes the staff members are state employees, but most are local volunteers who give their time to assist the pilgrims along their way. It is quite common for these places to provide a meal for their guests. These four-course meals are nutritious and inexpensive, typically costing around 10 Euros. Private albergues are owned and run as a business by private individuals or families. Cost varies, but expect to pay at least 10

Euros. Very often, these lodgings also have a number of private rooms.

On this, my first day of the Camino, I was on the road at six o'clock in the morning. I had spent the previous day in Pamplona checking out some of the sights, a portion of which was dedicated to trying to find the Camino trail. My time was well spent; I would soon discover that it is much easier to pick out the waymarks in daylight than in the dark. I was scarcely 15 minutes into my walk when I met Martina, a young woman from the Czech Republic who would become my very first walking partner. We reached an easy pace and walked side by side for 15 kilometres.

The morning was quite cool–around 12 degrees Celsius–but ideal for walking. The scenery, as we looked back toward Pamplona, was stunning. There were two very long climbs on this section of the Camino, which were easily manageable. Most walkers, myself included, found the descents much more difficult than the ascents. The footing was very tricky, with steep, rocky paths. Walking sticks are virtually essential for people my age in order to help with balance while navigating the terrain.

I stopped at cafés in small villages for breakfast and lunch. Breakfast consisted of a fresh chocolate croissant, American coffee and freshly squeezed orange juice. This was about to become habit-forming! The juice is simply exquisite as the oranges are processed in a machine before your eyes, resulting in the freshest end product imaginable. Lunch was a baguette filled with chorizo and tetilla cheese. Spain may not be as well known for its cheeses as some other countries, but I found them all extremely tasty. This was washed down with a cold beer, making a combination I would repeat many times along the way!

Martina and I parted company at Alto del Perdón. I was to discover later that the Camino has its own code: you walk intermittently with other people, and you can always sense when it is time to go your separate ways. Walking the Camino alone is recommended, as this provides each walker with maximum flexibility. During the day, I bumped into a couple of guys from Boston. One of them was only into his third day of walking (from Saint-Jean-Pied-de-Port) and his blisters were already debilitating. I also met Eric from Denmark, three folks from California, and Erica from Germany. It was endlessly fascinating to meet so many people from so many countries on my very first day of the walk.

Toward the end of my day I caught up to Raul, who is from Finland, but currently lives in Amsterdam. He was a quiet but very interesting chap. As we passed through several vineyards, he told me about his son's winemaking business. I was wearing a bright red fanny pack, which Raul made fun of persistently for the next few hours. The last hundred metres to our albergue were straight uphill. We managed to get a small and rather private room with only two sets of bunks. In an adjacent room with probably a dozen or more bunk beds, we could hear someone having an afternoon nap. It was my first (and definitely not last) taste of snoring on the trail. Raul and I chuckled, thinking of the poor people who would have to endure that guy for an entire night.

We decided to procure a beverage at a café at the bottom of the town, preemptively rewarding ourselves for the inevitable uphill walk back to our lodgings. We had scarcely toasted each other when Raul delivered what may have been the classic line of the entire trip. I had been chatting him up for two hours, thinking that he might be a subject for an interview for my book. "Len, We are comfortable with silence in Finland." Never had I been so politely told to shut up! The second beer was consumed in total silence.

I experienced my first of many communal meals that evening. There were about eight other pilgrims sitting around the table. We were given a bowl of tasty soup along with several different fresh, crusty breads. The main course was a dish comprised of prawns and chickpeas. One nice dessert and several glasses of red

3

wine later, we retired for a long night's sleep. The most typical Spanish dessert you will find on almost any menu (including albergues) is flan. This simple dessert is made from milk or cream, whole eggs and sugar and sets to a wobbly, jelly-like consistency. It is topped with a caramel sauce or syrup.

There was one other table of walkers adjacent to us who appeared to be having a great time as well. Partway through their meal, they were joined by two seemingly exhausted and distraught women. Indeed, they had every right to feel this way. They had missed a waymark and had veered off-course for three hours before getting back on the trail.

Day one couldn't have gone much better. Only three of the four beds in our room were occupied when we turned off the lights, my feet felt fine and I was delighted to have finally started my Camino. I was just dozing off when our door opened and a latecomer to the hostel meandered in and quickly got into his bunk. It only took him about thirty seconds to fall asleep and another minute to begin snoring. It's not hyperbole when I say that he was no ordinary snorer. This guy might have been a world champion. The sleepless night that ensued gave me plenty of time to reflect on our smugness earlier when we were feeling pity for the pilgrims in the adjacent dorm. I was soon to discover that having people snore in a large room is substantially less annoying than in closed quarters.

Martina

Martina is a young woman from the Czech Republic. For 10 years, she was a member of the Czech Republic Army. Her last three years before leaving the military were spent as a flight attendant, and she was able to see a lot of the world.

4

Recently, while traveling alone in Africa, she decided to part ways with her boyfriend.

Martina has suffered from depression, has had eating disorders, and alcohol problems and was a heavy smoker.

She decided to take a long walk to try and sort out the challenges she faces on a daily basis. She walked for three weeks through France before officially starting her Camino in Saint-Jean-Pied-de-Port.

She stopped smoking and drinking while on this epic voyage of self-discovery and feels that she is emerging from the darkness.

She is living with her mother as she charts a new path in her life.

Camino Tip #1: Follow the Yellow Arrows

By and large, the Camino is very well marked. Yellow arrow markers denote the path. These markers appear on the road, on the side of the road, bridges, walls, fences, telephone poles, rock outcrops, buildings, barns and the classic Camino concrete monuments, which also show the yellow scallop shell. In most places, especially in the small, rural villages, they are easy to spot. In large towns and cities, you really have to pay close attention because there are so many other signs that can distract a walker. Vigilance is crucial. Fellow pilgrims are very good to flag down someone who has missed a marker and is going the wrong way.

Chapter 2 – Cirauqui to Los Arcos

35k/48,282 Steps

The path from Cirauqui to Estella (approximately 14 kilometres) is relatively flat, save for the challenging footing at the beginning of the trek. I wouldn't suggest doing this in the dark. The town of Estella bears one of the most attractive offerings on the trail: one of the local wineries (Bodegas Irache) has an outdoor spigot, which dispenses free red wine! The Camino offers several alternate routes for those seeking either more adventure or solitude, as they are typically less travelled. One such path is just outside of Estella. There is a good climb up to Villamayor de Monjardín. There are some long hauls through vineyards and open country; one's water supply must always be topped up when walking a stretch like this. Los Arcos has a wonderful open air plaza near the church, which is a great meeting place for pilgrims.

I was pretty groggy after a sleepless night cohabitating with an elite international snorer in our small room. It was also very chilly. I had been told that the morning would be cool, but I wasn't expecting two degrees! I pulled out one of my pairs of socks and used them as mittens as I headed out the door. I quickly realized the importance of having walking poles as I began the treacherous exit from Cirauqui. Despite the degree of difficulty on the path it was a spectacular, sun-drenched morning and I was able to enjoy the scenery once I reached the bottom of the hill.

I passed through the city of Estella mid-morning. One quickly loses all sense of time on a trip such as this. It is not uncommon to hear the sound of church bells in Spain as every village, town and city has at least one church. In many of the smaller locales, you can grab a rope and ring the bells yourself. The local people must find this amusing for the first few hours of the day! The steady peeling of the bells reminded me that it was indeed Sunday and worshippers were being harkened.

The church is perched on a hill (they all seem to be on the highest piece of land in every community) and the Camino passes it directly. This is one of the many wine regions of Spain, and on the opposite side of the road is the Bodegas Irache winery. I noticed a small lineup at the winery, but I didn't see one at the church. This is the winery with the outdoor spigot and Camino participants (and one suspects some thirsty locals!) are welcome to help themselves to free red wine. Many people could be seen emptying their water bottles and helping themselves to the fruit of the vine despite the relatively early hour.

It was here that I met Jan, Aleksandra, Magdalena and Ray. The first three are a group of friends in their twenties whose paths I would cross several times in the next three weeks.

Leaving Estella on my own, I made a right turn and spotted the now familiar yellow arrow designating the trail. Within minutes I was traversing a lovely path through the woods. The trail narrowed and I realized from my breathing that I was going uphill. I sipped red wine and listened to the sound of birds chirping in the trees. The higher I went, the more rugged the path became. I also noticed that there wasn't a single pilgrim to be seen. I finally emerged from the woods and came upon a clearing, which revealed a stunning vista. It seemed like I could see forever, but way off in the distance I could faintly make out the main highway. *Odd*, I thought, as I was certain that the trail ran on the opposite side of this road. A quick glance at my guidebook revealed that I had indeed followed the road less travelled, taking one of the many alternate routes that the Camino provides.

I wasn't disappointed.

The combination of a long climb and a depleted wine supply resulted in my taking a seat on a large stone. I took in the paradise that engulfed me and I felt like I was the only person on the planet, such was the solitude. I will be eternally grateful for my choice not to follow the normal trail and the subsequent discovery of this gem.

But, as I was soon to find out, one is never alone on the Camino. While pondering my place in the universe, I happened to look skyward and noticed a dozen hawks flying directly overhead. My first instinct was that they were there to keep watch over me. As the glow of the wine was subsiding, I had another thought: maybe they were waiting to pick over my bones if I happened to stumble and fall!

The alternate route eventually connected to the main trail in a small village. I had lunch with Pablo and Nano, a Russsian couple now living in the United States. She is a former world-class skier and he is a holistic health practitioner. When I explained my neck and back issues, Nano stood up and showed me some exercises that keep her own pain issues at bay. After they left, I stood up and tried one of these exercises. I got some funny looks from other peregrinos (another name for pilgrims), who surely must have thought that I was suffering the ill effects of the sun.

As I was leaving the village I caught up to Nano, who was standing on a bridge with her cell phone to her ear. I rarely saw anyone actually on the trail who used a cellphone during the walking part of the day. Nano called me over. "You must speak with momma." Momma was her octogenarian mother living in Moscow. After a lovely three-minute chat I was on my way, marvelling at technology. Here I was, on a small path in rural Spain, talking to a woman from Russia.

The rest of the walk to Los Arcos wound through agricultural land and wineries. It was a beautiful day, with temperatures rising and a breeze at my back.

On the outskirts of Los Arcos, I came upon six high-spirited women who were doing the Camino together. I didn't need to guess their home country, as they spoke with a charming and familiar Irish lilt. When I discovered that they were from Dublin I started singing *Molly Malone,* and the seven of us strode into the city arm in arm.

My accommodations in Los Arcos were less than stellar. The room with ten beds was dirty and the bathroom and shower area were even worse. When I was shown to my bed by the proprietor, I noticed that the single bunk beside me was just a few short inches from my lower bunk. A couple from California was among my new neighbors. I started a conversation with them and was telling them about the aural horrors of my first albugue experience the previous night when there was a decided pause in the conversation. I was informed by the wife of my bunk mate, not three inches away, that her husband had serious snoring problems. She didn't lie; it was a night to forget.

The main plaza was packed with fellow hikers. After getting my lodgings sorted out, I returned to the square and found Jan, Aleksandra, Magdalena and Ray. We had pizza and red wine and shared stories from our day on the trail.

Aleksandra Ferek

Aleksandra is a 28-year-old woman from southern Poland. She is both a lawyer and an architect who dreamed about walking the Camino for many years. The Camino represents an opportunity for a religious and spiritual experience for Aleksandra, who grew up Catholic. She was traveling with one of her best friends and felt that the Camino would provide an adventure in a safe, welcoming environment.

9

Because she and her friend were traveling with a tent, they would have a lot of flexibility and freedom. Being able to share the journey with a close friend is a unique opportunity.

Aleksandra felt that the Camino would allow her to be who she is and find something in herself that she lost several years ago.

Magdalena Popinska

Magdalena is a 28-year-old software programmer from Poland. She also has a background in banking and decided to do the Camino with a good friend from home. She wanted to explore a new country on foot and to have the time to think about her life. In her words, she said "I might find my way."

For Magdalena, the best thing about the Camino is meeting new people and making new friends. She found, for the most part, that people on the Camino are caring and compassionate people. Because she was carrying a very heavy backpack, a fellow walker offered to switch his lighter pack with her to give her a break. The kindness of strangers was demonstrated on more than one occasion when people offered to help tend to her blisters.

Tenting with her best friend presented challenges but overall, the experience was very positive.

"The Camino taught me to be aware and to exercise caution."

She hopes to do another Camino sometime in the future.

Jan Bader

Jan is a 28-year-old man from Heidelberg, Germany. His background is in IT and Economics. His long-term goal is to become a writer but plans to resume his studies later this year.

The Camino was a journey of discovery for Jan, and he wanted to see how he fares traveling on his own. His father passed away four years ago and he was carrying a stone from home to leave at the Cruz de Ferro (the Iron Cross). The Cruz de Ferro is a monument at one of the highest elevations on the Camino, resting 1504m above sea level and consisting of a tall pole with a cross on top. People from all over the world come to this monument, carrying a stone from their home country to leave at the base of the cross. In many cases this gesture is to remember a loved one who has died. Like so many people on the Camino, Jan had overcome personal hurdles and was hoping that the Camino could provide him with some insights into his future.

Jan discovered that people are very friendly and easy to meet on the Camino.

He is also blessed with a very keen sense of humour, which was on full display as he marched across Spain.

Ray Mooney

Ray Mooney spent his early life in Limerick, Ireland, but for the past sixty years has lived in England. His wife died of cancer when she was only 35, leaving Ray to look after two young children. A police officer for 25 years, Ray went to Lourdes, France, with his family before his wife's death and it changed the course of his life. They all experienced unconditional love from the people they met in Lourdes so much so that he has been back with his children dozens of times since, often accompanying groups of young people.

A little over a year ago, Ray was diagnosed with prostate cancer. With his cancer in remission, Ray decided to walk the Camino this year. "I was always interested in doing a long walk and the Camino has given me the chance to celebrate my recovery from cancer," he explained. Ray has been impressed by the warmth and depth of the conversations with fellow walkers. "The camaraderie and respect for fellow travelers is something to behold. People reveal their innermost feelings on the Camino in a spirit of trust and openness."

Ray's walk has also raised funds to support Prostate Cancer UK and The Diocese of Arundel and Brighton Lourdes Pilgrimage.

*"Faith, fun, friendship and food." Ray experienced
this and much more on his "celebration of life"
walk across Spain.*

Camino Tip #2 : Bring Earplugs

You can choose to stay in private rooms throughout the entire Camino with some advanced planning, but if you want to experience the true pilgrim experience, you will spend many nights at an albergue. If you are a light sleeper, you may want to bring along earplugs, as snoring is an occupational hazard. I found that after a few days I got used to it and normally after a long day of walking, a communal meal and a few glasses of wine, sleep will eventually find you.

Chapter 3 – Los Arcos to Logroño

27.8k/38,422 Steps

This section of the Camino features one of Spain's notable wine regions, known as La Rioja. Local wineries, called bodegas, dot the landscape, from small traditional cellars to major commercial producers. Many consider La Rioja to be Spain's biggest and best wine destination. The region produces approximately 300 million litres of wine per year. The trail runs through farmland scattered with an abundance of vineyards. There is one small climb that provides some lovely vistas. Like most places in Spain, the city of Logroño boasts a large cathedral called Concatedral de Santa María de la Redonda.

I hadn't done much research on the weather before coming to Spain and had mainly looked at daytime averages. Had I paid more attention, I wouldn't have been surprised to discover that it was one degree Celsius outside when I left the albergue at sunrise. I passed a huge flock of sheep grazing in the pasture, and ahead of me on the road I could hear someone singing at the top of their lungs. I'm not certain of the language, but the song sounded lovely.

I consciously tried to walk slower on this day but it seems that I only have one gear when I'm walking alone. A familiar figure loomed in the distance; I soon pulled up alongside Raul and said good morning. We walked in silence for a few kilometres!

About 10 kilometres outside of Logroño, I met up with a man from France. He was going at a pretty good clip so I decided to walk with him for a while. Luc Bidaud had already been walking for five weeks, mostly in France. He had a lot on his mind. Between his broken English and my broken French, we were able to piece together quite a nice conversation.

Near Logroño we met up with Hannah, a young student from Cologne, Germany. She is an Environmental Studies Masters student. Living very close to the borders of The Netherlands and Belgium, she can bicycle to these countries quite easily on Sundays, when many shops in Cologne are closed.

After securing my lodgings for the night at Santiago Apostol, I wandered over to the main plaza to share a beer and stories with Luc, Hannah and Hillary, a woman originally from Wisconsin but now living in Northern France. Like so many of us, Hillary was having issues with her feet and had already been in Logroño for a day of rest. As I was to discover, a handful of people never make it to Santiago de Compostela (Santiago), the ultimate destination city of the Camino, because of injuries. There were rumours flying around that someone had actually died of a heart attack at Alto de Perdón just a few hours after I had been there.

There was a lot of banter at the communal meal. It seemed that everybody was dealing with some kind of physical issue after only a handful of days on the trail. I was sitting across the table from Kristina, a woman from Iceland. She'd somehow managed to lose a toenail on day one in the Pyrenees and had also suffered severe sunburns to her face and arms that same day in the unseasonably warm weather. A few days earlier, walkers had been taken off the same mountain because of a snowstorm. Camino hikers are warned– justifiably so–about the fickleness of the weather in the Pyrenees.

Luc Bidaud

Luc is a 52-year-old technical illustrator from Saint-Malo-du-Bois in France. As an industrial designer, he "imagines machines". The father of three girls, he considers himself a workaholic. He has come to the Camino to see if he can figure out a way to get some balance in his life.

He actually started his Camino in France on April 2, 2019, and by the end of his Camino he will have walked nearly 2,500 kilometers. His walk began in the snow and rain. He was concerned at first about where he would stay and how he would handle such a long walk. He was also worried about spending so much time alone.

"I am at a crossroads. I can't keep living as I have been. I need to find a better balance between work and family and must find time for myself as well. I need a change but am not sure what this will be. I don't know what I want to do but I know what I don't want to do."

Hannah Eichentopf

Hannah was born in Germany and currently lives in the city of Essen. She is a university student in the field of Resources Engineering focusing on Circuit Economy and Waste Management.

Having started her studies in 2012, Hannah felt that it was time to take a break. "Up to this point in my life, I felt that I was always doing things to please others. I felt the pressure and gradually over time, I changed. I didn't laugh as much as I used to and was often sad without reason."

The Camino seemed to be a good place to go just to be outside, go for a long walk and ponder her future. She went to Spain without a lot of expectations. "The Camino gave so much to me. I realized that I could have a positive effect on other people. I learned to laugh again. I learned to simply do things without thinking what others thought about me. And I met these wonderful people on the Camino."

Hannah had initially only planned to do a portion of the walk from Saint-Jean-Pied-de-Port to León, but the trip back to Germany filled her with sadness. She spent a week with family and friends back home but the pull of the Camino was too strong. She travelled to Porto, Portugal and did part of the Portuguese Camino so that she could meet her Camino family in Santiago. She also walked to Finisterra and Muxía and then went back to Sahagún and walked to Santiago again. Not quite finished, she walked from Zamora to Ourense on the Via de la Plata, another one of the Camino trails. In total, Hannah walked a total of 1500k on her multiple Camino walks.

"I returned to the Camino because I felt my experience had been incomplete. I wanted to extra time to spend with friends and think about what I really wanted to do with my life. This experience has been the best time of my life so far."

Camino Tip #3: If You're Over the Age of Sixty, Use Walking Poles

I wasn't sure about the usefulness of walking poles until the first day of my walk. On flat stretches, there's really no need for poles. You can simply hold them in your hands, although many older people use them to maintain a steady gait, favouring neither side of their bodies. Going uphill, especially on rocky terrain, walking poles are your friend, helping you to dig in for better traction. Going downhill, walking poles arc an essential piece of gear. They help you to keep your balance and navigate uneven ground.

Chapter 4 – Logroño to Azofra

35k/49,270 Steps

There's so much history on the Camino, as pilgrims have been walking these trails for centuries. On this stage of the journey, we encountered the first lake at Parque de la Grajera. Further up the road is Alto de la Grajera, the high point along this stretch that provides walkers with a panoramic view of Logroño. The town of Nájera was once the capital of the kingdom of Navarre. Apparently, a lot of royal figures are buried in this town. Azofra, like so many other small villages in Northen Spain, relies heavily on the Camino to keep it from dying.

I am an early bird, and have quickly discovered that many other walkers like to hit the road before the sun comes up. Unfortunately I did not purchase the popular head lamps worn by people wanting to start their walk in the dark, however the flashlight feature on an IPhone works perfectly well. The albergue started to come to life at four-thirty on this particular morning. Logroño, with its university, is a fairly large city, boasting in excess of 150,000 citizens.

As mentioned in an earlier Camino tip, while waymarks with the distinct yellow arrows are very easy to spot in smaller towns and villages, they can be less obvious in the cities where signs of all description are abundant, competing for a pilgrim's attention. Today was a good example of this. I found myself wandering around, a bit disoriented. I wasn't the only one. I teamed up with about six others and we collectively managed to find our way out of the city into the countryside.

An hour into my walk I met up with Marco Almeida, a 36 year-old man from Lisbon, Portugal. He told me that he was walking the Camino in the spirit of thanksgiving. Never having been to Portugal, I quizzed Marco about his country and a few hours later I decided that I would go to Porto (his recommendation) for a few days of rest after completion of the Camino.

I ate an excellent breakfast in Navarrete. Exiting the city, I heard someone whistling at me. It was a distinct whistle, one you might hear when you see someone stylish walking by. I also heard the all too familiar refrain of "Buen Camino". This was repeated three times. In my 67 years on this planet, no one has ever whistled at me. I was feeling quite chuffed until something caught my eye: in the first floor window of a building sat a parrot. The owners had trained the green bird to whistle and greet people. I was momentarily despondent that my secret admirer was from the bird kingdom, but my disappointment quickly turned to laughter.

I spent some time alone and caught up with Tracy, a fellow baby boomer. Tracy is from Australia and had recently experienced several life-altering events. She was a very successful businessperson until her marriage ended, resulting in her losing almost everything. Her father and brother had both committed suicide and she was estranged from virtually her entire family. She was understandably feeling quite lost; I gave her a hug, which was the best I could offer.

Everyone on the Camino is carrying a knapsack and some kind of personal baggage.

On the outskirts of Nájera, I met up with Linda and Kate from Twin Falls, Idaho. They were surprised to hear that I actually knew where that was. I told them about passing through their city a few years back on a trip with my son, Peter. We needed gas and food and took a five kilometre detour into Twin Falls. We quickly realized that this city is located on the banks of the Snake River. On

September 8, 1974, legendary stunt man Evel Knievel attempted to cross the Snake River Canyon (from one side of the river to the other) on a motorcycle. It didn't go so well, but it certainly put Twin Falls on the map.

Linda had recently become a widow. She'd sold her home and didn't know what she was going to do next. Kate had a serious car accident years ago, resulting in multiple injuries and excruciating pain for years afterwards. Recently, through treatments, her pain had dissipated, enabling her to walk the Camino. I offered to buy them a beer, as the weather had turned quite hot, and we stopped at a Chinese restaurant. They had picnicked an hour earlier and weren't hungry, so I kept it simple and ordered a combo plate. Several minutes and one misunderstanding later, three combination plates now dotted our table. I didn't have the heart to tell the young waitress to take the other two plates back to the kitchen, so my new friends from Twin Falls did the honorable thing and ate the other two portions. We all had a good laugh.

The three of us walked together to Azofra on a very warm afternoon. Our pace was deliberately slow, which was fine with me as this was the end of a 35k day.

I had preemptively booked accommodations on this day, something I did occasionally when I knew I had a long day of walking ahead of me. La Plaza was a bit pricey for a pilgrim, but it was well worth it. After getting cleaned up, I wandered down to the Sevilla bar and had a brew with four Americans. Three were from Port Angeles, a city in northern Washington State just across the strait from Victoria, BC, a place I had visited numerous times back in the 1970s. The fourth man was from Minnesota.

I had dinner outdoors with Matteo (not his real name) from Italy. Having struggled both physically and mentally in the early days of the Camino, he was now hitting his stride.

21

Back in my room, I made a clothing decision. For the first four days of my walk, I had worn an old pair of black running pants. They worked great for the early hours in the day when there was a chill in the air but once the sun came out, they were too hot. Because they were tattered anyway, I tossed them in a garbage can, lightening my load. I found out many days later that this rash move was ill advised!

Marco Almeida

Marco is 36 and lives in Lisbon, Portugal, with his wife and two small children. His wife and one-year-old son both nearly died at the time of the birth. He named his son Santiago. He had done several short Camino walks before but finally decided to do the entire Camino Frances. He considers himself a religious person and views this Camino as a pilgrimage of gratitude.

"The Camino speaks to you. It says that the road will be long and difficult, presenting many challenges, both physically and mentally. You will suffer pain and frustration. But the Camino rewards you with solitude, camaraderie and spectacular scenery to help you deal with adversity."

Camino tip #4: Don't Leave Large Cities Until Daybreak

Many pilgrims want to get an early start on the day. They get to spend some time in the quiet of early morning darkness and to witness beautiful sunrises. This is not a problem in smaller towns and villages, where getting back on the trail usually involves stepping outside your albergue and heading west. The path is easy to find, even without the yellow waymarks. While the streets are lit, finding the waymarks can be very tricky. If you feel compelled to start your daily walk in the dark in these larger centres, hang around your alburgue until a fellow Camino hiker surfaces. Usually, two sets of eyes will do the trick.

Chapter 5 – Azofra to Villamayor del Río

33k/46,021 Steps

The first stretch of today's walk from Azofra to Santo Domingo de la Calzada is comprised of open farmland running adjacent to a major highway. Santo Domingo de la Calzada is situated on the banks of the Oja River. Its name refers to its founder, Dominic de la Calzada, who built a hospital, bridge and hotel here for pilgrims along the French Way. The cathedral is named after him, and he was known as the one who constructed and improved roads in the area. As a testament to his work, roads in Spain are called calzadas.

After passing through the town of Grañón, one crosses into the region known as Castilla Y León. This vast area of approximately 95,000 square kilometres is comprised of nine separate provinces, including three that are on the Camino: Burgos, Palencia and León.

I was obviously getting accustomed to the snoring in the hostels, as I wound up sleeping in. I got going around seven o'clock that morning and early in the walk I met up with Regina Martens from Porto, Portugal. This was her fifth Camino but her first on the French Way.

The wind came up from the west mid-morning and it began blowing a gale. Reports late in the day showed wind speeds of up to 50 miles per hour, slightly less than a hurricane. It would turn out to be a very difficult day of walking.

24

As I exited one of the many small towns that dot the landscape, I heard a young woman singing, which is not uncommon. *What* she was singing caught my attention, though. *What Do You Do with a Drunken Sailor* is a sea shanty whose origins trace back to Ireland. The actual music was a traditional Irish dance and march tune called *Óró sé do bheatha bhaile*. In many western countries, this is a song sung at lively house parties.

I pulled up alongside her and joined in. She spun around and gave me a big smile. Katerina from Stockholm looked to be in her twenties and her walking partner, Wim, was a sixty-something man from the Netherlands. They had met at an airport in France and had decided to walk together. I decided to walk with them for the next stretch. I soon discovered that this couple was made up of the fastest walkers on the Camino, hands down. They were the first people who actually walked faster than me!

It was all that I could do to keep up with them for the next 10 kilometres, which was mostly uphill into the ever-stiffening wind. I watched in wonder as Katerina swooped and soared like a bird while walking. She danced and sang and displayed an exuberance rarely witnessed on the Camino. Walking beside the busy N120 highway, she exhorted the drivers of 18-wheelers to honk their horns. Most complied. We stopped at a hillside café for a bite to eat. I hadn't said a word to either of them for over two hours. It is not that we were unfriendly; the wind was simply so loud that you couldn't hear someone even a few feet away. I asked Katerina why she appeared so happy.

"I came here to have fun."

Enough said.

At this same resting area, I met Agnes from Budapest, Hungary, and Matteo, with whom I had dined the previous evening. Agnes teaches psychology at a university in Budapest. I decided to walk with this couple and bid farewell to Wim and Katerina. I never saw them again, which comes as no surprise. I had previously booked a room in Redecilla Del Camino but was enjoying my company so much that I changed plans and soldiered on with Matteo and Agnes. Shortly after leaving Redecilla, Matteo twisted his ankle, not an uncommon experience due to the frequency of uneven ground on the Camino. He wasn't able to continue and decided to seek medical attention.

Agnes and I walked in silence. We met up with three women from South Africa who were headed for the small village of Villamayor del Río. They, along with Agnes, had a reservation at the San Luis de Francia albergue. Luckily, I was able to get a room that included dinner and breakfast for 16 Euros. My good fortune continued, as I was the only male guest. My eight new female friends and I shared a meal and many laughs.

There was no heat in the albergue. I shared a room with Marie, a septuagenarian from France. I put on nearly every piece of clothing I owned and grabbed a second blanket. As I lay awake shivering, too cold to sleep, I couldn't hear Marie breathing. I initially feared that she had frozen to death, but I needn't have worried; just when my own sleep arrived in the wee hours of the morning, Marie began to snore. For the first time on the Camino I welcomed the sound, relieved that she hadn't expired!

Regina Martens

Regina Martens is from Porto, Portugal. This is her fifth Camino but first Camino Frances. She works at a clothing store in Porto. She is an outdoors person and walks the Camino for personal, cultural and spiritual reasons.

"The universe speaks to me while I'm walking and I speak back. If you embrace the world, it will embrace you back. I pay attention to nature while I'm walking. You can learn a lot by just paying attention. The Camino gives me what I need."

Camino Tip #5: Bring a Thermal Sleeping Bag

When I left Canada, I opted not to take a sleeping bag. I had been told that every albergue provided blankets, which I would later discover is not always the case. Instead, I bought a lightweight sleeping bag liner to use as an extra sheet beneath me. Travellers are wary of bedbugs (I never saw one in 25 days) and having something between you and the sheets is comforting. Alas, a liner will not provide warmth. A lightweight thermal sleeping bag is a good thing to have.

Chapter 6 – Villamayor del Río to San Juan de Ortega

29k/44,363 Steps

The trail passes through Belorado on the way out of Villamayor del Río. This town has been here since the 12th century and is home to some historic churches and castles. There are steep cliffs bordering the town that encompass ancient cave dwellings. From Belorado, it is a long (15k), slow climb up to Mojapan. Today's destination was an old monastery in the town of San Juan de Ortega. This is on a remote part of the Camino, so you might want to book ahead. This former Augustinian monastery was built around 1150 AD and there certainly is a monastic feel to the place.

For the second day in a row I was slow off the mark, leaving my albergue around seven. Fatigue is definitely a factor; the long days of walking and patchy sleep tend to catch up after a while. And, as was the case with my fellow pilgrims, blisters had made an appearance on both of my feet.

A few hours into my walk, I met up with Marianne and John Taylor from San Juan Capistrano, California. We stuck together for a while and they told me that this journey signified the first year of their new marriage, even though they have been married for over 30 years!

I stopped for breakfast at a busy café. Lineups are common, but the staff at these places are extraordinarily competent at serving hungry walkers. The Camino provides crucial employment to many communities that appear, at times, to be all but abandoned. On this day, I needed something heartier than a croissant. One of the most popular breakfast items in Spain is tortilla de patatas. It is also known as tortilla Española, or Spanish omelet. The main ingredients are eggs and potatoes. Other ingredients can include onions and red or green peppers. While I didn't find this dish particularly tasty, it certainly was filling and provided much needed calories for the day's walk.

As I was carrying my breakfast to my table, my coffee slipped off my tray, landed on the tabletop and spilled over onto the floor. I found a roll of paper towel and started mopping up. As I was completing my housekeeping a man appeared before me, holding a fresh coffee. He had gone back and stood in line to get me my morning fix. People on the Camino are extremely kind and generous. *Gracias, amigo!*

Later that morning, I was passing through a small village and discovered that I was perilously low on cash. There are ATMs in large towns and cities, but these machines are nonexistent in rural areas. I met two women outside a café who immediately noticed the Canada flag on my hat. Teresa and Tracy are twin sisters from British Columbia, Canada. Knowing that I would not have quite enough money to cover expenses for the next 24 hours before arriving in Burgos, they loaned me some Euros. They didn't seem impressed when I told them I was a retired financial planner!

We decided to spend the rest of the day together. Teresa and Tracy had recently celebrated their 50th birthdays and had decided to mark the occasion by doing the Camino. The walk was demanding and the temperature was cool, which was a blessing in light of the many sharp inclines on this stretch. We shared stories and laughed for hours on end.

We arrived at the old monastery in San Juan de Ortega late in the day and were able to secure a room. The accommodations were quite Spartan; the communal meal that evening can only be described as a fuel stop. Another staple food in Spain is Sopa de Ajo, or bread and garlic soup. Prepared properly with lots of garlic and spices, this is a hearty soup, renowned throughout the country. On this night, with no other restaurant options, the soup had little to no flavour.

Luckily, the wine was plentiful.

After supper, while hanging out near the office of this albergue (the only place with a hint of internet connection), I met Hans from Germany. He offered me a cold beer from the nearby beer machine. I don't think the Augustinians had one of these in centuries past! Hans was having a difficult Camino and offered that he had spent much of the journey in tears. He told me about his troubled life. We would meet each other a few more times along the way.

Marianne Taylor

Marianne and her husband John are from San Juan Capistrano, California. Early in her career, she worked as a hairdresser but became interested in psychology and horticulture. She currently works with special needs children, doing horticultural work in her community.

Marianne's Camino was important as she was walking with her husband, John, a recovering alcoholic. It was an opportunity for the couple to start their marriage anew. This rebirth started in the Pyrenees and ended in Santiago. "The journey was fabulous and difficult," says Marianne.

Marianne felt that the Camino had three distinct phases: physical, emotional and spiritual. "We thought we had trained but the reality with altitude and distance, we were challenged with pain and exhaustion. The second level was emotional for me walking across the mesata as it reminded me of a difficult childhood. The final level was spiritual–thanking God for guiding us."

Marianne feels as though the Camino was very important for the couple's marriage. "We both let go of the past and started anew with a future of hope and restoration."

Camino Tip #6: Maintain Your Cash Supply

Beyond large towns or cities, getting cash is problematic, if not impossible. It is imperative to keep an eye on your cash supply, as rural Spain operates on a cash only basis, including albergues and cafés. After running low once, I always paid close attention and looked ahead to see where the next ATM might be located. The ATMs work flawlessly, but you need to be aware of how the Euros get converted to the currency of your country.

Chapter 7 – San Juan de Ortega to Burgos

26k/40,260 Steps

About an hour outside of San Juan de Ortega is the town of Atapuerca. The area has been declared a UNESCO World Heritage Site. Apparently, some of the earliest human remains ever discovered in Europe lie here and there are suggestions that the folks who lived here over a million years ago were cannibalistic! The walk on this particular day was fairly easy, with very few elevation changes. There are two different routes into the large, bustling city of Burgos. My own route took me through Villafría, an industrial suburb. This path cuts very close to the local airport and it takes more than an hour to actually get into the downtown core. This is definitely not one of the more scenic stretches of the Camino. Probably the most recognizable structure in the city is the Gothic Catedral de Santa María XIII. This church has also been designated a World Heritage Site. Burgos, with a population of about 180,000, was the seat of the Franco government until 1938. It was also the home of the warlord El Cid. He was a famous Spanish national folk hero, purported to be the embodiment of chivalry and virtue.

I was restless before dawn that morning and decided I would get on the road early. I headed out of the monastery and luckily for me, I had company. Wim and Katerina were getting ready for another day of Olympic-style walking. They seem to glide rather than merely walk, and at a very high tempo. They turned on their headlamps as we headed into a heavily forested area. I had already decided that this would be a contemplative day for me and that I would avoid engaging people actively for stories; the walk through the woods was very serene.

Of course, Wim and Katerina all but left me in their dust, but I was happy to have the company even though not a single word was exchanged on the trail, nor when we had breakfast together.

For close to six hours, I was alone with my own thoughts. I paid attention to the sights, sounds and smells provided by Mother Nature. As had happened a few times before, I could hear singing up ahead. It was the familiar Love Theme from Romeo and Juliet. The song was being sung by a 69-year-old man from South Korea. He had a lovely voice. His walking partner this day was a twentysomething guy from Madrid. As I was passing them, I belted out a verse and a chorus of *Farewell to Nova Scotia*. All three of us were grinning from ear to ear at this jovial exchange on the trail.

I hadn't paid much attention to the guidebook and only realized later in the day that there are two routes into Burgos. After a hearty lunch of a sandwich, garlic and bread soup and a chocolate éclair, I headed for the city via Vlillafría. The walk seemed interminable and was quite boring. There were factories galore and huge transport trucks coming and going from industrial warehouses.

Dark clouds gathered overhead and for the first time on my trip, rain was threatening. I had booked a room at the Hotel Alda Cardeña and had managed to get an early check-in time, which was ideal, as I had been up early and the day's walk was quite short. I was using Google Maps to find my hotel, located well off the main trail and close to the city centre. Five minutes from the hotel, it started to spit; it was hardly worth getting out the rain gear. The skies opened up about 30 seconds after I entered the hotel lobby.

I approached the check-in counter with my passport and reservation confirmation number to discover that the clerk and I did not speak the same language. I tried to explain with gestures and an e-mail from the hotel confirming my early arrival that I wanted to get my room right away. "Not possible," came his reply. I tried again, futilely, to explain myself. "Not possible." I was resigned to sitting in the lobby for the next three hours; it was warm and dry, so all was not lost.

I took a seat on a couch across from the check-in counter. I watched the clerk shuffle papers and look at his computer monitor several times. I felt a hint of optimism as he summoned me and handed me a key to my room. I was doubly delighted a short time later, when I was able to ask a new clerk about getting my laundry done. For a very small fee (six Euros), I had a fresh stash of socks and underwear, the most crucial pieces of clothing on this trip.

On a subsequent trip to the front desk, I noticed two walkers checking in. I watched them enter the hotel. They were moving, shall we say, *gingerly*, carrying fairly substantial backpacks. They had not secured an early check-in (!) and were faced with the prospect of a wait. I invited them up to my room to pass the time. Jan Barnes and her daughter, Mac, were walking the Camino together.

By late afternoon, we were all famished. A friend had recommended the Casa Pancho restaurant as a good place to eat. Jan and Mac had met a man from London earlier that day, Charles Eve, and had invited him to join us.

Even with Google Maps, the location of the restaurant caused us to go in circles. It was nondescript from the outside and even upon entry it looked rather plain. This was until they escorted us upstairs, where we were greeted by a staff dressed in formalwear. The tables were adorned with linen tablecloths. It had the distinct feel of a high-end restaurant and, indeed, it was. Opening the menu provided a small wave of sticker shock but after eating many ordinary, inexpensive meals, it seemed like a good time to splurge.

The food was magnificent. In 2013, Burgos was named the "Gastronomic Capital of Spain". Succulent salmon, seasoned chicken and many other wonderful vegetable dishes were consumed, along with glasses of strong red wine. The dessert tray was a work of art and we got to sample some of the finest and tastiest sweets

34

imaginable. Tarta de Santiago, tarta de queso, torrijas, miguelitos and flan were dispatched with haste!

Burgos is a stunningly beautiful city. If I walk the Camino again, I will make sure to include a rest stay so I can spend more time checking out the sights, sounds and food!

Jan Barnes

Jan was born in the San Francisco Bay area. She has spent much of her work life in the real estate business, including many years in Sedona, Arizona. She spent six years in management with Procter and Gamble but eventually chose to leave the corporate world. She also has a background in nutritional science and once spent 10 months in Switzerland studying animal nutrition.

After working many years in the corporate sphere and raising a family, Jan was seeking something more spiritual by walking the Camino. "I am wondering if I can find inspiration to discover the direction of the next part of my life," she explained.

She also wanted the opportunity to do the walk with her daughter, Mac, a chance for some mother-daughter bonding.

She realized that the Camino would be tough and has five pairs of walking shoes as evidence. Meeting other pilgrims has been the high point of the journey. "My heart was touched by the people I encountered. This was evidenced by how often you might come across someone you had talked to for a bit and hadn't seen for days. You rushed over, hugged them and greeted them like an old friend."

Like many pilgrims, Jan realized that people are more alike than different, regardless of where they call home. This is a hallmark of the Camino. "This is a validation that the human spirit is alive and well and that we are all truly connected."

Mac Barnes

Mac is a 21-year-old student at St. Lawrence University, Canton, New York, majoring in business and art with a minor in writing. She recently completed three months of study abroad in Cortona, Italy, with a focus on art and art history. She was using the Camino experience to gather stories for a project.

She decided to walk the Camino to keep her mom company. As an athlete playing university volleyball, she is used to the rigours of training, but it appears that nothing could have prepared her for the Camino. "I have been surprised at the toll that the Camino has taken on my body. I feel beat up. I have trained all my life and this is the first time that I've had blisters."

It appears that regardless of age, people walking the Camino are searching for direction in their lives. "I'm still trying to figure out what I'm going to do with my life."

Charles Eve

Charles is a retired investment banker from England, having worked for years with Goldman Sachs. He has always been interested in music, having sung in church choirs for years. He also played the French horn and is on the board of the London Philharmonic Orchestra. He is quite interested in architecture.

After retiring at the age of 58, he traveled to Uganda as a volunteer to see if he might discover what to do with the next chapter of his life. He refers to this as his "gap year"!

The Camino has presented numerous challenges. Charles was plagued with shin splints and had to stop several times to receive treatment.

Camino Tip #7: Walk Alone for a Day

While the Camino is best known as a place to meet and talk with people from every walk of life, sometimes you just have to be alone. You'll know instinctively when you need a day of silence. Most times you don't have to say anything; people can tell by your body language. Other times, people that you're walking with will simply say, "I need to be by myself for a while." Just being alone with your thoughts is relaxing and life-giving.

Chapter 8 – Burgos to Hontanas

31k/43,769 Steps

This portion of the Camino gives walkers a break from some of the more strenuous climbs through the mountains. The flat, open land of central and northern Spain is referred to as the Meseta. It stretches approximately 200 kilometres, beginning just after Burgos and ending near Astorga. The Meseta is renowned for its breadth, barren landscapes and sprawling skies. Covering this ground can be taxing but if serenity is what you're looking for, the Meseta will provide this in abundance. It is essential to carry a lot of water, as the weather on this plateau can be hot and dry, depending on the time of year. The small town of San Bol has an excellent café for the hungry traveller. Hontanas, a classic pilgrim village nestled in a valley, provides a welcome change in land formation after trekking for hours over the flatlands.

I left my hotel in Burgos at dawn and headed in the direction of the Camino. Because I had gone off the beaten path to find a bed the night before, I wasn't sure how to get back on the trail. I wandered around aimlessly for a good 30 minutes until I spotted a guy with a knapsack who seemed to know where he was going. I caught up to him, and after chatting for the next several hours I realized that I had picked the perfect person to lead me out of the city and on to the Meseta. Maty Amaya is from Argentina and has been traveling around the world for seven years.

We caught up to Jordi, a young man from Barcelona, and the three of us would spend the rest of the day together. It was a cool, overcast day, which was perfect for the long walk ahead.

I also met up with another Tracy, this time from Australia. She explained that she has suffered from chronic pain for years. She had an operation a year ago and feels so much better. When I asked her why she was doing the Camino, her answer was short and sweet. "Because I'm able." She made an observation a few days earlier when the trail ran parallel to a major highway: "There were billowing fields of wheat on my left and a major highway on my right. The path dissected the two. I had romanticism on my left and reality to my right. The path is an attempt to find balance between these competing forces."

Because of work commitments, Jordi could only do a portion of the Camino Frances. After only a few days of walking, he was having serious pain in one of his feet. He was limping badly so I gave him my walking poles. I literally dragged him into Hontanas, our refuge for the night.

Hontanas remains my favourite stop on the entire Camino, which has everything to do with its location. After walking the plains all day, it was something else to go down over a steep hill and find this hidden gem. We located an albergue called El Puntido, which was one of the cleanest and well run up to this point.

After getting cleaned up, I went out on to the patio of the Puntido's café and sat in the warm sunshine. I sat with Clementine (France), Lily (Russia), Noah (Western Sahara), Jordi (Barcelona) and Rami (Finland). We drank beer and shared stories from several continents. I was sitting beside Rami and was telling him of my plans to get a tattoo at the conclusion of my walk. Oddly enough, he had been contemplating the same thing. After our second drink, we made a solemn pact to follow through on our plan and agreed to send proof that we had actually kept our promise.

Before evening dinner, I walked a few blocks to a Catholic church. A few days earlier, I had heard the sad news from back home of the sudden, tragic death of a young basketball player. I

40

quietly entered the building as mass was being celebrated and lit a candle in memory of Andrew.

The communal meal that evening was excellent. The red wine was flowing and everyone in the room seemed in high spirits. I spotted a classical guitar in the corner and while dessert was being served, I played two songs: the traditional Maritime tune *Farewell to Nova Scotia* and John Denver's *Country Roads*. The latter is obviously popular, as several people in the room joined in.

All in all, this was a fantastic day. The landscape had brought a refreshing change of scenery and I had met some amazing people.

Maty Amaya

Maty was born and raised in Argentina. He was in the financial business for years but in 2012, when the Argentinian economy was in shambles, he lost his job and was quite depressed. He bought a bike and told his family that he needed to go for a long ride to clear his head. Seven years and 93,000 kilometres later, he's still on the move.

He has visited 40 countries and is doing the Camino for the seventh time. The previous six were on his bike, but this time he walked. The first time around, he was confused. He'd flown into Santiago wondering what all the fuss was about as pilgrims were ending their journey. He got on his bike and mistakenly drove to Saint-Jean-Pied-de-Port in the wrong direction. He did his first Camino backwards!

In December of 2017, he was biking through Italy around Christmas. A couple saw him on the side of the road, stranded in a blizzard. They took him in and gave him food and shelter for several days. A few years earlier, this couple had been in a horrific car accident. They were both in comas for nearly six months and when they awoke, they learned that their only two children had been killed in the accident. They gave Maty a stuffed animal, which he christened as Emilio, and which now travels the world with Maty firmly affixed to his knapsack.

The Italian couple plans to come to Spain to walk the final 100 kilometres with Maty and Emilio.

Maty has seen and done a lot as he travels with his bike, which weighs in at 90 kilograms fully loaded. He was stabbed in Central America and spent three weeks deep in the Amazon forest with tribal people, among other adventures. His next stops are in Africa and Asia.

"Anything is possible if you put your mind to it" has become his mantra.

Raimo Ojala

Raimo was born in Rovaniemi, Lapland, Arctic Circle, Finland. He now lives in Hameenkoski in southern Finland. He was a locksmith by trade and a partner in a lock company.

A few years ago, Raimo was watching a television program about a group from Finland that had walked the Camino. The thought of a long walk appealed to him but at the time, he was too busy with work. Once he retired and had time on his hands, he decided to head to Spain to walk the Camino.

"The entire Camino was an incredible experience. I met so many wonderful people and built new friendships with people from all over the world. Arriving in Santiago de Compostela and spending my final hours with friends is something I'll never forget. So much laughter, hugs and a few tears saying goodbye to people who shared the trail with me."

Along the walk, Raimo had been thinking about getting a tattoo to commemorate this epic event. In the town of Hontanas, he met Len MacDonald (yes, the author of this book!) on the patio of a bar at the albergue. When Len mentioned that he planned to get a tattoo, the two agreed to make a pact. "I always try and keep my word." In late June, Raimo got his tattoo, a permanent reminder of this great journey.

Camino Tip #8: Drink Lots of Water and Be Careful Drinking Water from Public Taps

Staying hydrated on a long walk is crucial. Even when you're not thirsty, it is advisable to keep drinking lots of fluids, especially water. Most modern backpacks come with a water bladder that can carry up to two litres. Some people buy bottled water and carry it affixed to their backpacks. Getting refills is relatively easy; any café is happy to to give you a top-up. A walker does, however, need to be very mindful of drinking from the many public taps along the trail. While most are clearly marked as "potable" or "non- potable", I witnessed firsthand the results of tainted water. Two friends became so ill along the trail that they had to take several days off to recover.

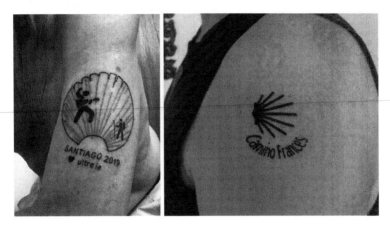

Chapter 9 – Hontanas to Frómista

35k/46,452 Steps

The Meseta continues. Castrojeriz is another town owing its present fortune to the past, as it was once a popular spot for early pilgrims to stop on their journey. The town was established in 974 AD and, at one time, had several hospitals. There is a fairly steep climb out of Castrojeriz up to Alto de Mostelares, which gives way to more flatlands. After passing through the town of Boadilla del Camino, you come upon a rather odd sight. There is a manmade canal, Canal de Castilla, which runs alongside the Camino for several kilometres. It was originally designed for irrigation and to transport goods. As you near Frómista, there are several locks on the canal. The locks are able to raise and lower water levels, enabling boats to pass through. At one time, there were fifty locks in operation. Frómista was once a significant exporter of wheat.

It was a very nippy one degree Celsius leaving Hontanas. I met up with Jan and his walking partner for the day, Frida, who is from Denmark. We would spend the whole day together continuing the long walk across the Meseta, and my feet were suffering as the blister count mounted. We passed through a village and saw a café advertising the "best coffee on the Camino." We stopped, and for once there was truth in advertising, as it was indeed superior coffee. While sitting in the café, I overheard some folks speaking English. They were from Tipperary, Ireland, which resulted in a few choruses of *It's a Long Way to Tipperary.*

One of the blisters was on the bottom of my foot and I couldn't see it clearly, so I asked Jan and Frida if they would take a look at my feet. Up to this point, I had simply been using pharmacy bandaids but soon became acquainted with Compeed, a brand of hydrocolloid gel plasters for treating blisters. My two friends got out their medical kits and after some quick first aid I was back on my feet and ready to go. I discovered over time that no amount of bandaging relieves the pain of walking 30 kilometres per day on blistered feet!

The ascent to Alto de Mostelares is one of the longest of the entire Camino. The three of us passed everyone over this three-kilometre stretch, which is a very demanding climb. The view at the top is spectacular. The Camino generally rewards you after it has punished you!

We stopped for lunch and noticed a couple of guys on horses. We found out that they were doing the entire Camino this way. Thinking about the terrain already covered, I wondered how the animals managed. I also thought how sore a person's butt would get sitting in the saddle all day long! I hadn't noticed any albergues with stables, but obviously there are places for these types of travellers.

About five kilometres outside of Frómista, our destination for the night, we passed several people dressed in period costumes. They had walked six kilometres to Frómista to take part in an historic re-enactment and were now on their way back home. It was a very warm afternoon and we marvelled at them travelling all this way to carry out this important local tradition.

Frida Rosenlund Falk Thoestesen

Frida was born in Denmark in 1994. She completed two years of university in Aalborg. At this time, she decided to take a break from her studies. She did a four-month stint in the military for the physical challenge and camaraderie. She was interested in the leadership aspect and applied for a program in this area with the military, but then decided that completing her university education was a priority.

She spent a few months in Bali doing yoga training and learning about meditation and self-awareness. She also witnessed firsthand a great deal of poverty and observed a culture of gratitude despite hardship. Prior to this, she was a self-proclaimed workaholic and during this training she tried to unlearn this character trait. She used the analogy of a handful of peanuts. "Rather than eat the whole handful, I learned to eat each peanut one at a time, savouring each piece. I discovered the joy in the small things of life."

She went hiking with her father in Nepal but the trip was cut short when he developed altitude sickness.

The Camino was an impulse decision. "People in Denmark are very aware of the Camino. I just decided one day to do the pilgrimage and booked my ticket without much thought. It just felt like the right thing to do." Her goal was to complete the Camino by just taking things a day at a time.

*She was surprised by the camaraderie and
fellowship on the trail. "I thought people would be
more inward looking, spiritual and contemplative.
I found it just the opposite. People were very open
and honest."*

*However, home is where the heart is. "I found out
how much I missed home and just being in one
place. Now, I really value being home."*

Camino Tip #9: Carry a Small Mirror

There are no beauty contests on the Camino, so don't let vanity get in your way! I do, however, suggest that you carry a small mirror. This is not used to apply makeup–the reflective surface can merely be used to check your feet for blisters. Sometimes blisters occur in awkward places; being able to see them clearly can help you decide whether they are far advanced enough to break them and bandage them up.

Chapter 10 – Frómista to Calzadilla de la Cueza

36k/47,995 Steps

The landscape on this section of the Camino could be fairly described as unremarkable, but that doesn't deter most walkers, as it's quite an easy stretch to traverse. The town of Villalcázar de Sirga is notable for having been one of the command centres for the Knights Templar back in the 1200s. The Knights Templar was a large organization of devout Christians who carried out a mission to protect European travellers visiting sites in the Holy Land during the medieval era while also carrying out military operations. On the outskirts of Carrión de los Condes, one can visit the historic remnants of San Zoilo Monasterio, which dates back to the 1100s. There are virtually no services in the long stretch between Carrión de Los Condes and the final destination of Calzadilla de la Cueza; I located a single pop-up café along the route but no water taps or toilets.

My walking partner from yesterday, Frida, and I were up and on the road early. It was a very cold morning. We had walked for a couple of hours and were both very hungry. According to the guidebook, the next significant town was at least an hour away. Just off the main trail, we spotted some walkers and discovered the small café, which had just opened for the day. Needless to say, we were overjoyed at this unexpected turn of events and enjoyed a wonderful breakfast of Spanish omelet, croissants, freshly squeezed orange juice and dark roast coffee. In the back yard were some farm animals, including donkeys and chickens. As we made our exit, the chickens came spilling around the corner to bid us adios and presumably to clean up our crumbs!

The long, empty 17k stretch ending in Calzadilla de la Cueza was a bit tedious. My feet were killing me. I even (naively) tried walking more softly. I figured if I put each foot down gently, it wouldn't hurt so much; this experiment lasted about fifteen seconds.

The town of Calzadilla had two albergues side by side. By late afternoon, the main bar was packed with fellow travellers. I sat with fellow walkers Felicity, Pia and Jakob and enjoyed a cold beer. Later that evening, I met an amazing family from Denmark.

Almost a year ago to the day, my mother died in her 92nd year. She grew up in Montreal in an Irish household and was a woman of incredible energy, an attribute that came in handy on the Camino, as I'm certain I got some of *that* DNA. When I checked into the hostel, my wide-brimmed Tilley hat was soaked with perspiration. I asked the check-in clerk if there might be a ball cap lying around that I could borrow, as I didn't want to sit outside in the hot sun with by bald head exposed to the elements. When he returned, he produced the sole hat that had been left some time ago by a pilgrim. I did a double-take when I saw the crest: a shamrock, the most well- known symbol of Ireland. I must admit to getting a few goosebumps. I was also a bit choked up. Of all the hats that might have been left behind, the only one was from Ireland.

While unpacking my bags after checking in, I realized I had somehow managed to lose my phone charger. This was hardly surprising, as my early morning exits are almost always executed in the dark and things are bound to go missing. I wasn't the least bit concerned, as I reckoned there might be an iPhone or two on the Camino. While having beers at the outdoor café, I simply asked in a loud voice for the loan of a charger and, not surprisingly, I had my phone charging in seconds. People on the Camino never hesitate to share.

One other notable thing about this particular albergue was the shower and toilet stall—they were *tiny*. I am not a particularly big person, but getting in and out of the shower (or toilet) required Houdini-esque theatrics. There wasn't anywhere to leave your clothes other than on the floor outside the shower stall, so if one was prudish in the least, this would have been off-putting. It was genuinely difficult to even turn around in the shower. I would hazard a guess that locals from the 11th and 12th century might have been a wee bit smaller than their modern counterparts!

Felicity Rose Sunderland Hall

Felicity was born in London, England. She moved to Montpelier, France, at the age of five. She is currently in her third year of university in Birmingham, England, where she is majoring in business, Spanish and Arabic. For the past year, she has been doing an internship in Valencia. She is working for a small company that designs luxury bathrooms.

Felicity has already faced some adversity in her young life. She has undergone three kidney operations but finds herself in good health these days.

Her parents met in Africa, so it was no surprise that Felicity traveled there in the fall of 2015 after her 18th birthday. She visited Mozambique, Zimbabwe, Zambia, Botswana and Namibia. She lived for three weeks with a Zulu family in South Africa. While there, she volunteered at a school. There was no common language but they managed to communicate very well. They gave her the Zulu name of Oxelele. She discovered that the Zulu people were warm, kind and generous. Returning home was a severe culture shock.

Ten years ago, her mother did the Camino. Felicity decided that it was time she took on this adventure, her improved health being a key determining factor.

She enjoys the sense of togetherness and notes that she never feels alone.

"I want a clean start. Nothing can hold me back. I am here to reconnect with myself and I am determined to finish the Camino."

After completing the Camino, Felicity had a few observations. "I was determined to prove to myself that I could physically do the Camino. I soon realized that it wasn't the physical aspect that was holding me back, but the mental part. My "mental weight" was actually harder to carry up a massive hill than my backpack. Doing the Camino was the best decision I could have ever made. I'm so grateful for all the blessings I have in my life, including the beautiful people I met along the way."

The Bang-Wolfsberg Family

After a year of military service in his early twenties, and in peak physical condition, Anders Wolfsberg decided to go for a long walk. He left Paris and walked to Santiago, a distance of approximately 2,500 kilometres. He also ran the Camino once, starting in Pamplona, a distance of 713k.

Anders and his wife, Tina Bang, both schoolteachers, had a dream of someday walking the Camino with their children, Vidar and Astrid. The children had seen the pictures from their father's previous Caminos and had become interested in doing the walk with their parents. The planning started in earnest two years ago, including arranging time off from school.

Denmark doesn't have a lot of mountains so most of the training, complete with backpacks, was on flat terrain. Anders knew that this would be challenging for the children, particularly the mental aspect of doing such a long walk. They started their Camino in Pamplona on April 24th, 2019. The plan was to combine 12 walking days with three rest days.

Almost three weeks into the journey, each member of the family had some observations. Vidar (age 9) commented that he was finding the distances long and the weather hot, but he was having fun being together with his family and not being in school! Astrid (age 13) was missing her friends back home, possibly the most challenging thing for a teenager who values her friendships. "I didn't realize how big the Camino would be. It is physically and mentally difficult."

Both Tina and Anders view the experience as partially spiritual and partially a chance to get out of the rat race. Not having to do the mundane day-to-day things has been a joy for them.

For Anders, doing the Camino with his family is a whole new experience. "The first two Caminos I did for myself. Now, my focus is on my family–to make sure that this is a good experience for them. It requires focus, concentration and planning."

The family's arrival in Santiago on June 6th in the pouring rain was somewhat anticlimactic. "We felt that our goal had already been accomplished while on the trail. We knew that we would miss the walking, the people on the road, the simple way of life and being close together with each other." The family was glad to get home and to stow this experience away in their mental backpacks.

"It is an experience that grows inside us still."

Camino Tip #10: Carry a Roll of Toilet Paper

If ever there was a stretch of the Camino where toilet paper just might be your best friend, the road to Calzadilla de la Cueza definitely comes to mind. Finding a bathroom is generally not an issue, as towns and villages are fairly close together, but every once in a while, especially if nature calls, you're going to have to find a place to answer that call. Privacy cannot be guaranteed, but when you gotta go…

Chapter 11 – Calzadilla de la Cueza to El Burgo Ranero

41k/53,000 Steps

Today's journey was the longest of my Camino. The terrain continued to be very flat as we crossed into Provincia de León and the town of Sahagún, which has historical significance. It contains some of the earliest examples of the Mudéjar style of architecture. Mudéjar refers to the large group of Muslims who remained in Iberia in the late medieval period, despite the Christian conquest. The destination on this day was El Burgo Ranero. This town once thrived on its wheat and wool industries but these days, it is primarily Camino traffic that keeps the place going.

I started my day with a cup of Russian coffee lovingly prepared in the large washroom/shower facility at Calzadilla de la Cueza by my friend Lily from St. Petersberg, Russia. It was definitely a heart starter! The night before, there had been one hundred pilgrims all sharing the same room in the albergue. It was a very warm night and sleep was at a premium.

People are very honest on the Camino, and Frida had indicated her desire to walk alone once the sun came up. We all enjoy a good chat but also have the need for solitude. Both can be accomplished very easily. Walking in wide open spaces with no artificial light provides a clear glimpse of the heavens. It was a spectacular starlit morning.

As I pulled ahead of Frida, I had this recurring thought: I had just met this person yesterday. We'd shared stories about our lives in complete openness and honesty. A bond was cemented, a unique friendship developed, and we parted ways. These chance encounters are very fleeting and often leave a person deflated because you know that, in all likelihood, you will probably never see your new friends again after the Camino.

My plan, as per usual, had been to have breakfast after the first two hours of walking. Instead, I wound up connecting with two walkers, Soren from Denmark and Enrica from Italy. They were going at quite a healthy clip and I'd decided to tag along. Soren is a super fit 65-year-old. He starts his days back home with water and lemon and doesn't have his first meal of the day until noon. He admitted that it was impossible to follow this regime on the Camino. Enrica is in her late twenties. The two have been walking together since the first day.

The conversation was lively and, before I knew it, I had covered 21 kilometres. It was only half past nine in the morning! This turned out to be a good thing on a day that was long and hot. We stopped for breakfast, where I must have consumed 2,000 calories. While I was eating, there was a tap on my shoulder. I was delighted to see Luc and Hannah, a couple of my walking mates from earlier in the journey. One of the great joys of the Camino is meeting up with people you haven't seen in days. These greetings, full of backslaps and hugs, often give the appearance of a reunion between long lost friends. They stopped long enough to say hello, and all four of my comrades eventually continued on without me as I hung back to do some foot repair.

By early afternoon, the temperature had crept up to 27 degrees. Thankfully there was some shade along the way, as there were trees every 10 yards or so. I stopped in Bercianos del Real Camino and quaffed the largest and chilliest beer I could find. My legs were quite badly burned, despite an application of sunscreen earlier in the day.

When I arrived in El Burgo Ranero that afternoon, I felt close to death. The last three hours of my 41k jaunt had been in 30 degree heat. Victor, a pleasant young man, checked me in, checked me out and determined that this wild-eyed Canadian was in desperate need of a beverage. He hurried off and returned with two frosty Estrellas. I could have hugged him. Actually, I did! He popped off the tops, we clinked bottles and I slaked my thirst.

After a second beer and a shower, I was in bad need of sustenance. Victor told me that the best restaurant in this tiny village was on the main street. It turned out to be the best and worst restaurant in town, as it was the *only* one!

Walking very gingerly on achy feet, I arrived at my destination to discover that the owners, a youngish couple in their thirties, were having a full scale war. Their small son was crying as the two went toe to toe in an epic verbal battle.

I regarded the action for a solid five minutes. I was deliriously hungry and the plastic flowers adorning my table were beginning to look appetizing.

The man and his son left and the woman, dabbing tears from her eyes, approached my table. I pointed to the menu board on the wall and ordered the chicken breast, along with a glass of red wine, and begged for the immediate delivery of some bread.

With hand gestures, she indicated that this particular entrée would take one hour. A wee bit exasperated, I pointed to the chalkboard once more and gestured broadly, indicating that she could choose my supper. Another interminable 10 minutes passed as delirium set in.

Eventually she approached my table with a plate of cheese, fresh baguette and a bottle of the finest red wine on the planet. I could have hugged her but decided discretion was the better part of valour in the restaurant's current emotional climate.

The food and drink nearly brought me to tears, such was their exquisite taste. The second course was a fresh salad of chilled prawns, tuna, tomatoes and onions, topped with a salad dressing of Spanish olive oil and balsamic vinegar. Had I kicked the bucket right then and there, I would have died happy.

As if this weren't enough, she then called me to the counter and presented several varieties of homemade sausage. I can't begin to describe how delectable these tasted when pan-fried.

She insisted I have ice cream for dessert, but I was too full of food (and bliss) to oblige.

This meal was easily the best 13 Euros I had spent during my time in Spain. To top it off, the owner walked me through a hallway to the back of the building so that she could show me her magnificent garden.

She kissed both of my cheeks and gave me the biggest hug imaginable. A potential nightmare had turned into a highlight of my Camino.

I went back to my room and slept like a baby.

Enrica Stucchi

Enrica is from Bergamo, Italy. She has a background as a language teacher (English and Italian) but recent events have caused her to ponder where the future might take her. With a varied skill set, she was trying to decide whether her vocation is in the arts (drawing and painting, writing, dancing, singing), the field of education or the tourism industry. The possibilities for her are endless.

With many personal challenges recently, she had been unable to focus clearly. Doing nothing wasn't an option, so she made travel plans to go to Saint-Jean-Pied-de-Port, the starting point for the Camino. This pilgrimage had been on her personal bucket list for some time.

The experience was very rewarding. She met people from all over the world, conversing in several languages. The physical exertion was life-giving, despite some painful injuries along the way. She loved being with other people but was at peace when she had time to walk alone. She enjoyed the small things that make the Camino special, like sharing meals with new friends or having a complete stranger help her with her medical needs, a common occurrence on the trail!

With her batteries recharged, she felt confident that the answers to her questions about the future would reveal themselves in due course.

Soren Krause Andersen

Soren is a retired businessman from Denmark. His early work career was in development, converting customer demands into product solutions. Prior to retirement three years ago he'd held several human resources positions, including coaching and competence management.

"My interest in development is an integrated part of my personal development. I continue to challenge my understanding of what I know."

When he retired, he decided to do two things: write a book about his beliefs and walk the French Camino. He recently completed his second Camino. "I was looking for inspiration as to what to do next with my writing and authorship." He received a lot of encouragement from fellow pilgrims to pursue this goal.

He discovered the uniqueness of the Camino, where people from around the world come together. He noted that fellow walkers were friendly and open-minded, and that there was a feeling of mutual acceptance across all boundaries.

"Try to imagine how the world would be if we all brought an equivalent strength with us back home. Conflicts between religions, nations...and so forth would vanish. What a perspective!"

Soren revealed that this year's Camino provided many great insights and had given him the inspiration he needed to move forward with his writing.

Camino Tip #11: Change Your Socks Partway Through the Day

First of all, buy good quality socks! I would recommend six pairs. Every day, halfway through your walk, remove your walking shoes and socks and air out your feet. Change into a fresh pair of socks. Dry socks will help minimize blisters. This will give you three days' worth of comfortable footwear.

Chapter 12 – El Burgo Ranero to León

38K/52,013 Steps

The early portion of this stage can best be summed up as a long meander across sprawling terrain. The senda, or pathway, is tree-lined in many places, providing bits of shade along the way. The town of Mansilla de la Mulas was once an important livestock centre but today it caters to pilgrims on the Camino. The city of León looms in the distance. Much of the second half of this walk runs alongside the busy N-601 highway.

Small things make a huge difference on the Camino. A good night's sleep and clean underwear rank somewhere near the top of the list. After yesterday's punishing walk, nine hours of uninterrupted sleep was the best medicine possible, although it did little for my aching feet. I awoke in the dark hours of the morning after having collapsed in a heap in my bed at seven o'clock the previous night, following an outstanding meal. While rooting through my knapsack, I discovered a pair of clean underwear. It's hard to believe that finding clean underwear could evoke such joy but on the Camino, you travel light and clothes tend to get recycled, as laundry facilities can be hard to find.

I left my lodgings and was greeted by the sounds of thousands of crickets in a nearby swampy area. Walking across the vast senda, I gazed heavenward at the billions of stars and watched an orangey moon descend as the sun was rising in the east. I didn't meet a single walker for 15 kilometres, the longest such stretch since I began my walk. Rather than feeling isolated and lonely, I felt calm and serene. It was quite spectacular, in an understated way.

I walked as quickly as I could. I knew I had another long day ahead of me, and I knew that it was going to be another scorcher. I stopped for lunch in the town of Arcahueja, about seven kilometres from León. I examined my feet and was able to determine that something was definitely amiss with the baby toe on my right foot. I couldn't see the full extent of the problem, but it certainly appeared infected.

While under the shade of an umbrella, I watched with great interest a procession beginning to form at a church next door. My initial assumption was a funeral, but many of the participants were dressed in colourful costumes. I was to discover that today, May 15th, was the feast day of St. Isidore, the patron saint of farmers. He was known for his piety. In extremely hot temperatures, the procession moved from one end of town to the other, with music and song. It was quite a spectacle after a day of seeing almost no living souls on the Camino.

It was hot when I left Arcahueja. The path that winds away from the town leads up a very long and quite steep hill. It was obvious that the heat was affecting other walkers, as I spotted several by the side of the trail gathering breath or becoming physically ill. Although not technically the most difficult climb of the Camino, the time of day, temperature and condition of my feet made this feel like an Everest climb. Cresting this hill, León could be seen in the distance.

The walk into León seemed interminable. It took quite a while to get from the outskirts to my final destination. Entering the downtown core, I met a young man who was doing an actual religious pilgrimage to Santiago, with the hope of determining whether or not he would become a priest.

The last two hundred metres to get to my hotel was straight uphill, the final insult after an exhausting and painful day on the Camino.

It rained hard that evening, preventing me from scouting out the city, but this was a blessing in disguise as it gave me a chance to put my feet up. The next day would be a much needed rest day.

An Act of Camino Kindness

Participants in the Camino are well known for acts of spontaneous kindness and generosity but sometimes, people will go to extraordinary lengths to assist a fellow pilgrim, as the following story illustrates.

On the second day of their Camino, Jan and Mac (see chapter 7) met up with three other walkers from their home country. The trio consisted of a married couple and their twenty-something son. They were all staying in the same albergue that night, and they exchanged contact information.

Terri (not her real name), the wife in the trio, fell and broke her ankle during her walk. They were able to track down a bus and transport her to a nearby town to be assessed. She was treated and sent to Sarria, where she received a cast, all but ending her dreams of finishing the Camino. Her son left and was able to track down Jan and Mac to inform them of the mishap.

With the news of Terri's injury, a new plan was suddenly hatched: Terri would taxi ahead each day with her crutches and meet the others at cafés along the way and, eventually, predetermined albergues.

A few days after the accident, Jan and Mac came upon a family with an older gentleman in a wheelchair being pushed by "a rather buff young body builder," and an idea was born. In the town of Melide, they were able to rent a wheelchair suitable for use in the outdoors and the five now set off together, traveling in a much different fashion.

Her husband, son and Mac were tasked with the job of wheeling Terri. They took turns pushing the wheelchair and restraining it on the downward slopes. Jan carried the crutches, which would be required at rest areas and at the end of the day. She was also a forerunner of sorts, scouting out the path ahead and removing any large stones, twigs or branches that could jam the wheels if not cleared. This odd-looking group attracted the attention of many walkers and they became the subject of countless Camino stories on social media. Many photos were taken and Terri became somewhat of a celebrity, even signing autographs!

The group literally rolled into Santiago in early June on a hot and muggy day. They should have been elated when they heard the skirl of the bagpipes in the great plaza, but they were all overheated and exhausted. After numerous selfies, the group headed off for a quiet evening at their hostel.

While this story is quite unusual, it speaks volumes about the spirit of the Camino.

Camino Tip #12: Pack Extra Underwear

Talking about undergarments is a delicate subject but on the Camino, every discussion is open and honest. Yes, it is easy enough to hand wash all of your clothes at virtually every albergue on the Camino but at the end of a long day, would you rather have a cold beer with friends or stand by a basin scrubbing your undies? I think six pairs of underwear would do the trick. I know that everyone on the Camino is, at some point in time, forced to re-use clothing, but there's just something about recycled underwear that holds little appeal.

Chapter 13 – León

Rest Day

Doing a long walk takes its toll on the body and the mind. Rest days become necessary in order to recharge the batteries. I decided that one of my rest days would be in the historic city of León. This metropolis, with a population of approximately 130,000, is the capital of the province of León. It is home to many churches and cathedrals, most notably the 13th century Gothic Catedral de Santa María de León. The city was founded as a military encampment around 29 BC. The Barrio Húmedo is the name given to the city's casco antiguo, or "old town". It is the "wet district", where the city's biggest concentration of bars, pubs, taverns and cafés is located.

Until this part of the trip, my breakfasts had been mostly the same, but being in a nice hotel in a large city I decided to indulge in the on-site breakfast. I've had many buffet breakfasts over the years, but this one will definitely be a list-topper. They had croissants fresh out of the oven (plain and chocolate), a variety of sumptuous cheeses, ham, chorizo, cream puffs, bread, cereal, orange juice (freshly squeezed), fresh coffee, an assortment of fruit and doughnuts. This "all you can eat" bonanza cost the princely sum of five Euros; needless to say, I went for seconds the next day.

While I was carb loading, I said good morning to a couple at the next table. "Hello" turned into a fascinating 90-minute conversation with Bernd and Rosario from Costa Rica.

It was a beautiful morning as I gingerly took my first steps of the day. One of my priorities was to find someone who could look at my feet, or replace them! I purposely walked slowly through the streets of León. I spent an hour or so wandering through the mammoth Catedral de Santa María de León. The grandeur of the place was jaw-dropping, particularly the stained glass. It also caused me to wonder about organized religion and how many of these historic churches and cathedrals were built with the blood, sweat and money of the working class.

I stopped in at a small bookstore. There hadn't been many opportunities to read lately, so I thought I'd grab something for the rest of the walk or for the plane ride home. I chose a critique of *Don Quixote*, the work of Spain's most famed author, Cervantes. While roaming through the English language section, I bumped into an English-speaking woman who just happened to be from Claresholm, Alberta, Canada. The early part of her Camino had been anything but smooth sailing. Her bags were lost by the airline and she'd had to wait three days to get them. She'd gotten sick on the trail and had lost a few more days. To add insult to injury, she'd hyperextended her leg and hurt the top of her foot. Her comment? "Everything is going great." She said she was a bit beat up but that in recent years she has developed mental toughness while training for Iron Man competitions.

Having lunch in a bar in the Barrio Húmedo district, I met a few familiar faces, including Jakob from Michigan and my walking partner near Hontanas, Jordi. I was very surprised to see Jordi, recalling how badly he'd been doing several days prior to this. He admitted that he'd had to take a bus for a few stages to get back on track.

I had a wonderful afternoon siesta and, feeling refreshed, headed back out to track down some supplies at a sporting goods store. The clerk was extremely helpful and a funny guy. We really hit it off. When I told him about my battered feet, he suggested a reputable podiatrist one street over.

I entered the premises of a business office that provided both physiotherapy and podiatry. The place was spotless and had a very pleasant atmosphere, with classical music playing in the background.

The podiatrist was a young man dressed immaculately in professional attire. He took me into a case room. It was extremely well equipped. At least, that's how it appeared to me. It didn't take him long to determine that a blister had formed under the toenail of my baby toe and was indeed infected. He removed several instruments from sterilized packages, which was a comfort. For 45 minutes, he worked away. There was no discomfort whatsoever. He gave me a topical cream with instructions to use it for three days. If the toe didn't heal, it would require an antibiotic. I couldn't believe the bill. For basically saving my baby toe, all he asked was five Euros.

I was so relieved to have my feet taken care of–and with such excellent service–that I treated myself to a glass of red wine and a dish of olives at one of the thousand or so sidewalk cafés in "the Barrio."

I did a lot of thinking that day. Until the previous day, I had been moving along the Camino at a pretty fast clip. With my feet in such bad shape, I was concerned about not being able to finish the walk due to the infection worsening. Ultimately, I determined that not finishing, while disappointing, wasn't going to be a big deal. Starting the following day, I would dial back the pace and possibly even follow the suggested stages in the John Brierley Camino guide. Instead of pounding out 31k per day on average, I would now be looking at something closer to 22 kilometres, which would reduce my walking by about two hours per day.

I did some calculations and even with the reduced mileage count, I would still arrive in Santiago long before my flight back to Canada on June 7th.

The big question before going to bed was whether or not the toe would respond to the treatment and how it would feel inside my walking shoes.

Bernd and Rosario

Bernd grew up in Germany. He worked as an investment banker for 20 years with one of the world's biggest and most well-known financial institutions. He decided that he needed a break from work and went with his then wife and two children, ages 10 and 13, for a sailing trip around the world. While aboard the sailboat, the boys continued their education through a specialized correspondence course. Two years turned into four, and the family ended up in Costa Rica.

Bernd had an epiphany of sorts. "If you walked in flip flops for four years, how can you go back to wearing dress shoes?" He also came to realize the dark side of the banking business. "When you're "inside the box", you can't see outside the box. You're trying to help rich people avoid taxes."

Bernd decided to sell everything back home and relocate to Costa Rica. After four years of travel, the boys wanted a more normal life. His wife wanted to return to Germany and this was when the couple separated.

With all of his corporate knowledge, he was able to get involved in some start-up companies in Costa Rica. He still has an ownership stake in one company but a year ago, he decided to move on to the next chapter of his life and enjoy retirement.

Rosario is from Costa Rica, one of 14 siblings. Family is extremely important in her country and the girls were expected to work on the family farm until they were married. She went to university and got a degree in business, with a focus on banking and finance. She is the credit manager for a lighting company. In 2004, she met Bernd online and eventually they got married.

Bernd has done the Camino before and this time they are only walking the stages that they really want to do.

"The Camino should be about pleasure, not pain!"

Jordi Silvente Villa

Jordi is a young man from Badalona, a city about ten minutes away from Barcelona, Spain. He is a tattoo artist and also sells drawings commercially.

Jordi has always been interested in the outdoors and has an adventurous streak in him. He especially likes mountain sports. He realizes that many people do the Camino for religious reasons but he does not include himself in their numbers. "I have some issues with organized religion," he says.

Upon completing his Camino he mentioned the great atmosphere and the good vibes. "I met so many interesting people along the way. We all had the same goal but we were a mixture of generations." He loved the ever-changing landscape and the variety of food.

"This has been one of the best experiences of my life and I hope that this is the first of many Caminos."

Monica Smuda

Monica currently lives in Claresholm, Alberta, Canada. She spent five years in Comox, Vancouver Island, B.C. in what she calls her "island paradise". Prior to that she worked for Ford Motor Company for many years.

She initially walked the Camino in 2016 and took seven weeks to complete the walk. Shortly thereafter, her life changed drastically upon suffering the fallout of a relationship that ended egregiously. She decided to return to Spain in 2019 to try and sort some things out and get herself back on the track to a healthier lifestyle. She had been a triathlete in a previous life and knew the importance of staying physically active.

Her adventure got off to an inauspicious start. Her backpack arrived three days late, delaying the start of her walk. She had a bout of illness on the trail, which temporarily derailed her, and she hyperextended her leg, causing a painful foot injury.

Unlike her previous Camino, which was more in line with a spiritual experience, this Camino was more about the physical. "Walking every day with pilgrims in Spain seemed to give me the loving boost I needed to get myself back on track physically, mentally and emotionally. I felt my self-esteem recovering daily in remarkable ways."

Like so many other pilgrims, meeting people from other countries and forging new friendships was a highlight. Her mother's hometown was in Germany and Monica had learned the language and local dialect. "On the Camino, I also had a lot of fun speaking German with many pilgrims."

"I brought far more stress with me on this Camino than on the previous one. Now that I have completed my Camino, I am definitely feeling healthier and far more optimistic and confident. I am even in the pool regularly now, swimming my usual 2k, which I haven't done in years."

Camino Tip #13: Go at Your Own Pace

You hear it every day on the Camino: *Go at your own pace.* Everyone who takes this journey will spend time walking with other people. It is never a problem to walk with someone slower than you, but caution should be taken when one attempts to keep up with

74

gazelles. It's commonly agreed upon that setting a pace beyond your comfort zone is asking for trouble, and this is precisely why many experienced pilgrims suggest walking the Camino alone and setting your own timetable. Trying to mimic someone else simply doesn't work. It is *your* Camino, after all.

Chapter 14 – León to Villadangos del Páramo

21k/31,642 Steps

It is quite conceivable that this is one of the more bleak stretches of the entire Camino once you pass León. If you keep your eyes peeled, you may catch a glimpse of one of Gaudi's architectural masterpieces, the neo-Gothic palace Casa Botines. Getting out of León takes quite a while and care must be taken to follow the waymarks. The main route runs alongside the N-120 for virtually the entire way. You cross the Bernesga River (Rio Bernesga) on a 16th century stone bridge, head west and follow the highway. There is an alternate route that one can take to avoid the highway. It takes you to the town of Villar de Mazarife.

This was the first day of my amended plan. I decided to sleep in, as my day was only going to involve four hours of walking, provided that my baby toe was cooperative. I waited until the pharmacies opened and visited five of them trying to get a prescription for antibiotics, just in case the topical ointment didn't work.

One of my brothers is a doctor and I thought an e-mail from him with instructions would suffice to get me a prescription. Wrong! None of the pharmacies had any of the medicine in stock and even if they did, it would require a written prescription from a local doctor. The earliest that I could possibly get all of this done was in 24 hours. I decided not to wait around.

I got a message from Jan, who was in the city. I met him in front of the cathedral in the main plaza and we headed out of the city together. It took the better part of an hour to get to the outskirts.

After the previous two days of hot weather, it was quite cool but still sunny. We stopped in an industrial park and had one of the best glasses of orange juice you could imagine at a roadside food stall. Less than two hours into our walk, Jan had to stop, complaining of gastrointestinal problems. He felt certain that he drank some contaminated water from a public fountain.

As I continued on, I was far more interested in my feet than landscapes, castles and churches. Knowing I didn't have to walk for endless hours, I took my time and walked at a leisurely pace. I felt good and, as I had on so many previous days, I grew stronger as the day went on.

I arrived at my albergue in Villadangos del Páramo mid-afternoon. The place was huge and in one room of 30 bunkbeds, there were only a handful of people. The facilities were excellent, with clean bathrooms, hot showers, a laundry room and a place to cook your own food. They even had a machine where you could purchase bottles of wine or beer.

The communal dining area was busy with the handful of other pilgrims who had checked in. Everyone was journaling, checking their guide books for the next day's walk and accessing social media.

At one table there were six of us, three on either side. Klaus, from Germany, showed me how to use the coin-operated beer machine. The first mouthful startled me. It was lemon flavoured. I did the honourable thing and drank it before buying a real beer. Others were drinking fine red wine from León. Guido, from Italy, was sitting to my right, and a woman from Germany was on my left. Three other fellow walkers faced us on the other side of the table.

As I was enjoying my beverage, the German lady asked if she could borrow a guidebook. Guido reached across in front of me, thrusting the book to the grateful pilgrim. However, so enchanted was he with this woman that he kept his arm extended after passing her the book. As a result, his armpit was in my face and his arm was between me and my beer.

The people across from me were watching with grins on their faces. I delicately passed my hand under Guido's arm and brought it up and over in order to get a mouthful of ale. Guido remained oblivious to my predicament. I started pointing at his armpit to the three people across the table to jokingly suggest that he had body odour (he did not). This little charade continued for a full five minutes. When our tablemates' grins finally erupted into laughter, Guido finally realized that he was the subject of everyone's attention. We all had a great chuckle.

Later during dinner, I struck up a conversation with a retired Anglican minister from Northern Ontario and a computer programmer from London, England. She looked to be around my age and the other fellow was in his twenties. I asked the minister if she felt safe traveling alone. "I'm on a mission of trust" was her reply. No question that her Camino was a spiritual journey. If she visits every church on the Camino, they might need to send out a search party for her later this fall.

We continued on to have an illuminating and candid discussion about organized religion, spirituality, the afterlife, same-sex marriage and more.

My friend, Enrica, was spending the night at the same facility. She was still having all kinds of medical issues, yet was kind enough to look at my feet. She seemed to think that my toe was healing as she applied the sterile bandages that had been given to me by the podiatrist.

A phrase heard often on the Camino goes like this: "The Camino gives you what you need and not what you want." Everyone who comes to do this walk arrives with expectations. It may not provide everything that you expected but it certainly delivers what you need, when you need it.

78

One year ago today, my mother died. Before going to bed, I watched a video my seven siblings and myself singing one of Mom's favourite hymns, *Abide With Me*.

Klaus Hubner

Klaus was born in Bensheim, Germany. He worked in the health insurance field and took the opportunity to retire early. He obviously loves his home city. "I was born in Bensheim, have lived my life in Bensheim and will die in Bensheim."

Prior to retirement, doing the Camino wasn't possible because of work commitments. He had read a lot about the Camino and had hoped one day to be able to do it. In 2018, the family suffered a devastating loss. His granddaughter, Amaya, died 10 short days after her birth. "I decided to do the Camino and deposit a stone at Cruz de Ferro in her memory." It was a very difficult time for the family.

In the early stages of the walk, he was passing through the city of Pamplona with his new friend and soon to be frequent walking partner, Guido. They were trying to find their bearings and were looking for the familiar waymarks. The very first street that they walked down was called Amaya. He instantly found himself collapsed and sobbing in the arms of his Italian friend.

"I met so many wonderful people on the Camino. Some of them I only saw for a day and others for the entire Camino." Klaus admits that he shed many tears along the trail. Some were tears of joy and some were tears of sadness, realizing that these chance meetings with total strangers were fleeting and that he would likely never see them again. Such is the Camino.

At the Iron Cross, he deposited his stone in memory of Amaya.

Immediately upon returning home, he vowed that he wouldn't return to Spain for another long walk. "After all the pain and being away from my family for such a long period of time, I couldn't see myself doing another Camino." But with many new friendships forged on the journey, Klaus is now thinking that another Camino might just be in his future.

Camino Tip #14: If You Set a Blistering Pace, Your Blisters Will Multiply

I haven't researched this topic carefully but I believe the combination of long walks, uneven ground, moisture (sweat) and walking pace all contribute to blisters. Most walkers are not used to walking 20-30k per day in their normal lives, so it is hardly surprising that blisters are the most common problem on the Camino. If you try and go too far, too fast, you likely increase the odds of getting multiple blisters.

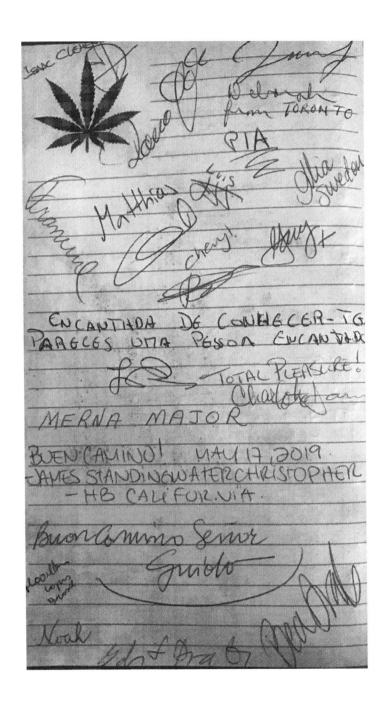

ISAAC CLEMENT

Deborah
from TORONTO

PIA

Matthias Luis Mia Sweden

cheryl!

ENCANTHDA DE CONHECER-TG
PARECES UMA PESSOA ENCANTADA

TOTAL PLEASURE!
Charlotte Jam

MERNA MAJOR

BUEN CAMINO! MAY 17, 2019
JAMES STANDINGWATER CHRISTOPHER
— HB CALIFORNIA.

Buon Camino Senor
Guido

Noah

82

Chapter 15 – Villadangos del Páramo to Astorga

30k/40,892 Steps

On the Camino, you will cross many medieval stone bridges, but none are quite like Puente de Órbigo. Situated in the municipality of Hospital de Órbigo, this bridge is the site of a famous jousting tournament that took place in 1434. In that year, the Leonese knight, Suero de Quiñones, held a tournament in which he or one of his companions challenged all men of equal rank who wished to cross the bridge here to a jousting tournament. He was holding the bridge in the name of unrequited love. The tournament lasted almost a month, during which time the knight is claimed to have broken 300 lances, all in the name of chivalry!

The city of Astorga was very important in its heyday because of its strategic location at the convergence of several roads. Probably the most famous landmark is the Spanish architect Gaudi's Palacio Episcopal, or the Bishop's Palace. It was built in the late 1800s in the neo-Gothic style. It houses a museum with artifacts and historical notes on the many Roman roads that meet in Astorga.

Earlier in my travels, I had ditched the only pair of long pants I had with me: running pants that I'd owned for more than 10 years. They were tattered and torn and weren't serving any useful purpose. I wore them in the mornings when it was cool but not long after the sun came up, as they were too warm. Looking ahead in the guidebook and talking with fellow walkers, I knew that we would be heading back into the mountains in the next few days. Knowing that I was heading to Astorga, a larger city, I decided that I should buy another pair of jogging pants upon arrival.

I walked briskly for two hours on a very cold morning. I stopped at a café and rather than my normal light breakfast, I loaded up and ate just about everything on the menu, including an éclair, which I simply couldn't resist. I was sitting by a window and spied my friend Luc, who came in and joined me. He looked quite fatigued, which was hardly surprising, as he has been walking since June 2nd (see Chapter 3). Luc appeared to be somewhat stressed out, and he told me that he'd made plans to stop at a monastery for a few days later in the trip to catch his breath and collect his thoughts.

It was not an easy day of walking. It was windy, and walking into a headwind always requires more energy. There were a lot of long hills and the paths were cluttered by rocks, making the footing quite tricky.

The highlight of the day was crossing the Puente de Órbigo. The bridge itself is quite amazing, possessing 17 arches, but it is the history of this bridge that fascinates pilgrims and tourists alike. The city of Hospital de Órbigo continues to host an annual jousting tournament in the first week of June each year. It appeared that preparations were well underway as I crossed the ancient bridge. When it is celebrated, the residents of Hospital de Órbigo put on medieval clothing and recreate typical 15th century scenes. The town swarms with knights armed with swords and shields, monks, peasants, archers and maidens. The fiesta, or festival, lasts several days. I vowed to come back here one year to take part, but only as a spectator–I will leave my lance at home!

My albergue in Astorga, Siervas de María, was an old convent. It was massive and, not surprisingly, had a distinct religious feel to it. The hallways were full of historical remnants. I immediately noticed that the convent was very cool, temperature-wise. Checking in, I was very surprised to discover that they didn't provide blankets, a first for me on the Camino. They informed me that the fear of bedbugs had resulted in the "no blanket" policy. I immediately turned all of my attention and energies to getting those long-legged pants.

I was directed to a small room with only two bunkbeds. From earlier experience, I knew that this was a double-edged sword. My roommates, Noah (Germany), Francisco (Brazil) and Gary (Wisconsin, USA) turned out to be great guys. We all had snacks in our backpacks and we shared them with one another.

I did a quick Google search and was somewhat alarmed to discover that many businesses in the area are closed on Mondays, including all the sporting goods stores. I imagined going to bed in shorts and no blankets and having to have someone chip the ice off me in the morning. I headed out and miraculously found the one sports store that was actually open. Beggars can't be choosers at a time like this. I purchased a pair of thermal running pants, which seemed like a bargain at 52 Euros under the circumstances.

I had a huge dinner mid-afternoon: fresh crusty breads, seafood paella, meatballs, all the red wine I could drink (within respectability) and dessert. When I'd had my fill, I left the café and wandered the streets of Astorga. I was tempted to visit the Gaudi museum, but wandering around a museum after 30 kilometres on my feet didn't hold a lot of appeal. As with many of the other locations I had visited along the way, Astorga would be on my list of places to stay longer on a subsequent Camino.

Early that evening, I sat in a bar and wrote for an hour in my journal. I did this because a) there wasn't a suitable place to write at the albergue; b) the bar wasn't cold and c) the convent didn't have a beer machine. I was getting up to leave (seriously!) when a familiar face entered the bar. It was Jakob from Michigan. He took a booth with a young Italian man that I had seen many times before as well as a man from Austria, and they invited me to join them.

The man from Austria was wearing a sleeveless shirt, exposing his impressive muscles. I stared at his biceps and saw an amazing Camino tattoo. I am known to have bouts of compulsiveness and right at that very moment, I decided that I would get a similar–if not identical–tattoo at the conclusion of my walk. He told me that he'd gotten got his tattoo in Santiago on a previous Camino walk. He even had the name and address of the tattoo artist. The name, evoking rebellion and darkness, was just what I was looking for: Old Skull Tattoo and Piercing. I was pretty stoked leaving the bar.

Late in the evening, I returned to my room. The old convent felt even colder, as the temperature had dropped several degrees. I laid out my super thin sleeping bag liner and then started piling on layers of clothing, including my running jacket. As I lay there shivering, I thought about the convent and the Sisters and wondered if they had been run out of town for not paying their heating bills!

Mercifully, none of my roommates snored.

Rev. Gary Manning

Rev. Gary lives outside of Milwaukee, Wisconsin, USA. He is an Episcopal clergyperson serving a congregation of 430 people.

Seven years ago, Gary watched the movie The Way and knew immediately that someday he would walk the Camino. With a two-month sabbatical on the horizon, he'd decided that this was a good time to make the pilgrimage. "I knew that I needed the opportunity to slow down so that my soul could catch up with my day-to-day life. My hope was that by walking The Way, it would give my body something to do while my usually very chatty mind could relax a bit."

While doing the Camino was primarily for religious reasons, he also felt that the walk would provide gifts of personal discovery, the experience of being in an entirely different culture and the opportunity to speak with fellow pilgrims from all over the world.

As is the case for so many others the Cruz de Ferro was the highlight of Rev. Gary's Camino.

"Since I began this Camino, I've seen my share of rocks! I've walked atop them, tripped over them and stumbled upon them. And, all over the place, my fellow pilgrims have written messages on rocks, spelled out words with rocks and stacked rocks in all sorts of configurations.

"I arrived at the Cross just after sunrise. The waning moon was setting in the west. The temperature was perfect. The wind was calm. I have been trying to be a better me since I was 12 years old so now, a half a century later, at a spot in Spain, I tossed away my constant need to be better, and the accompanying affliction of self-deprecation."

Like so many pilgrims before him, Gary felt just a bit lighter, having deposited his burdens at the foot of the Cross.

Camino Tip # 15: If You Don't Bring a Sleeping Bag, Bring a Pair of Long Johns

If you have read tip #5, you can ignore the rest of this, as you will have decided to take a sleeping bag. Remember, a sleeping bag adds to the weight of your backpack. If you haven't taken a sleeping bag, I would suggest a good pair of old fashioned long johns. As I discovered, not every albergue has blankets and when you encounter cold nights, especially in the mountains, wearing something warm is important. It can be difficult enough to sleep with all the other distractions of your surroundings, but being cold on top of this will almost guarantee a sleepless night.

Chapter 16 — Astorga to Foncebadón

26k/38,856 Steps

After many days of relatively level ground, this segment of the trail presents the walker with some challenging climbs. Most of this stretch is spent walking up long hills and the highest points on the Camino occur here. If you are looking ahead to Cruz de Ferro and want to arrive there at sunrise, the village of Foncebadón is a good place to stop, as it is only two kilometres away from this famous Camino landmark. In the village of Rabanal del Camino, you might hear the sounds of Gregorian chanting, as a group of monks has taken up residence in the community.

I didn't have to get dressed this particular morning, as I was already wearing just about every stitch of clothing I owned in order to stay warm. I was up very early and chomping at the bit to get walking and raise my body temperature. On my way out, I was somewhat surprised to see a handful of walkers lingering in the lobby area of the albergue. Normally, the early birds pack up and go; lingering is not in their DNA. There is, however, an explanation for this anomaly. This particular albergue locks it doors at night and doesn't open them until six o'clock in the morning. While one can understand part of the logic (to prevent non-pilgrims from wandering in at all times of the night), my thoughts turned to fire safety. What if a blaze broke out? It would certainly warm the place up, but in this respect I felt that locking the doors posed a very serious hazard.

My feet were brutally sore that morning and every step was painful. The Camino teaches perspective and I turned my thoughts to those people suffering from cancer and other diseases. Their pain is permanent, while mine is temporary. I trudged on.

90

I stopped in the village of Rabanal del Camino to check my feet and have some sustenance. A familiar voice was blasting from an outdoor speaker; it was none other than Johnny Cash singing *I Walk the Line*. How appropriate! On my way to get a drink, I stopped and sang along with Johnny. Several other pilgrims on the patio joined in. I hung out here for the better part of an hour, listening to several more of his tunes. The influence of music is quite amazing, especially country music. It doesn't seem to matter which country you're in; you'll frequently hear the old Country and Western classics, sometimes in the most unexpected places!

There was a huge blister on my heel that needed lancing, so I got out my medical kit and performed this delicate operation. This was the same heel that had received attention before. Blisters on top of blisters were a new phenomenon for me–and one I wouldn't care to experience again.

A secondary paved road ran alongside the main trail and I decided to walk on the road to ease the pressure of walking on uneven ground. It was very chilly heading into the mountains. I met Yung 1 from South Korea, who found it exceedingly cold. For many years, he was an office worker in the busy city of Seoul but finally got tired of the rat race and bought a farm in the countryside. I was tempted to say that life in the capital city sounded Seoul-destroying!

The last five kilometres to Foncebadón were laid out entirely on a rocky incline. There was an abundance of wildflowers and the scenery was breathtaking. Earlier in the day, I had purchased a milk chocolate bar that was approximately the size of a VW Beetle. I stopped partway up the mountain and sat down on a rock to get a blast of energy. As I was unwrapping the chocolate bar, a young man came strolling along. His name was George and he was from Hungary. I couldn't resist a quip. "Are you Hungary, George?" I could hear my children groan all the way back in Canada. We each started off modestly, taking one small square of chocolate. Ten minutes later, there was nothing but an empty wrapper and two severely sugar high walkers. George could not believe his good fortune. This chance meeting lasted all of 15 minutes. George was young and walked quickly; I never saw him again but I suspect that he repeated this story to his friends back home more than once.

The weather was simply spectacular as I entered Foncebadón. After checking in, I wandered the small village and found a great pizza shop. The two guys working there were straight out of the 1960s: their dress and their language had "hippie" written all over it. While I was in the process of ordering my pizza, unbeknownst to me, one of the guys had pulled out a bullhorn and a speaker and proceeded to emit the most obnoxious blaring noise one could imagine. I wondered if an enemy army was coming over the mountain, but no—I simply hadn't noticed their outdoor patio at the rear of the shop. The alarm was a signal to outdoor diners that their pizza was ready.

While waiting for my pizza to cook, I went out back and sat at a table with Bea and Edit Drab from Sweden. We had a wonderful chat.

The pizza was excellent and the two hippies were super guys. I'll make sure to stop here again the next time I do the Camino.

I stayed at an albergue that night that is worth noting. If there's such thing as a five-star hostel, the Convento del Camino is it. The rooms were small and clean and included a private bathroom. The meal was above average and, for maybe the first night ever, no one in my room snored.

On the Camino, staying in hostels comes with the package. If you're a light sleeper or can't handle communal bathrooms and less than deluxe meals, this might not be for you. Every once in a while you get a surprise, and today was one of them. I will definitely bookmark this for my next Camino.

Bea and Edit Drab

Bea Drab and her mother, Edit, are from southern Sweden. Bea started her career as a nurse but decided to become a doctor. She is beginning a two-year internship. Edit is a retired nurse, having spent much of her work career caring for elderly patients with dementia. This is their third Camino together.

Edit's husband passed away a year ago, and she and her daughter felt that by doing the Camino they could move on with their lives. Edit, who feels that her normal life has changed forever, is coping with the loneliness of her new reality. This Camino is an opportunity for her to figure out what's next in her life. "I am looking for a sign or some inspiration. The answers might come from complete strangers."

From previous experience, Bea feels that the Camino has three distinct phases. "Some people do the Camino in pieces over a period of years. I think you need to do it all at once. The first part of the walk is physical. The second is mental and the third is spiritual."

While dealing with the emotional pain of the loss of a loved one, Bea and Edit are reaching their quota of physical pain this third time around. "We've had our share of blisters, knee pain and ankle issues," says Bea. But she says that the pain is nothing comparable to the joy. "A blister won't be painful in a few weeks. Life is like this. Learn to embrace the pain."

*Walking the Camino is a great equalizer. No
matter your country of birth or occupation, the
Camino treats everyone the same. "We are all
dealing with similar issues on this journey. The
Camino has a way of bringing us back to the
simple things of life. You meet people from all over
the world that you would otherwise never meet.
You have unexpected support all around you,"
says Bea.*

Camino Tip #16: Bring a Pair of Sandals

At the end of a long day of walking, removing your shoes is a highlight. The last thing you want to do is spend one extra minute with these too-familiar companions. Bring along a pair of sandals– preferably flip flops–that you can wear around the albergue and also in the shower room. With so many people using washroom and shower facilities, going barefoot comes with some risk of getting an infection. The last thing a walker needs to add to their discomfort is athlete's foot.

Chapter 17 – Foncebadón to Ponferrada

27k/41,902 Steps

Today's walk began with a stop at The Cruz de Ferro, one of the most important points on the Camino, next to the Santiago and Finisterra.

I must admit that I hadn't done much research on the Cruz de Ferro before I came to Spain, but as I got closer to the cross, I became aware that this was a very important stop for pilgrims. Like many others who had stayed in Foncebadón the previous night, I had timed my exit from the village so that I would arrive at the cross as the sun rose. Six of us headed out in darkness. At the end of the village, there were two roads and no waymarks. This was the only time on the Camino that "The Way" wasn't obvious. Through the magic of GPS, we all came to agree to take the path on our left.

It only took 30 minutes to climb the mountain. I stayed at the cross long enough to witness several walkers deposit their rocks in the ever-expanding pile. This was obviously a very emotional time for many pilgrims. The next 13 kilometres were also uphill, leading to the highest point on the Camino, near Manjarin, at 1,515 metres above sea level. The weather could not have been better and the scenery was simply exquisite, with a dizzying array of beautiful wildflowers, mist-covered mountains and sparkling valleys of every shade of green imaginable.

While the climb was strenuous, the descent, simply put, was brutal. The trail to the village of El Acebo was steep and very uneven. On blistered feet, every step produced winces of agony. My walking poles were absolutely critical. I tried to visualize doing this section of the Camino on a rainy day. It would not be impossible, but

I guessed it would probably produce many injuries. I had breakfast in El Acebo. Once again, the Camino gave me what I needed: fresh baked goods. Most cafés along the Camino have a fairly standard breakfast menu, but this place had a variety of delectable cakes and squares. I sampled more than one of them and was on my way.

After a tough stretch dealing with yet more blisters, I staggered into the town of Molinaseca. It was now hot outside. I noticed that there was very little chitchat among the pilgrims having lunch. I could tell that the Camino was taking its toll on people's psyches as well as their bodies. After a well-deserved rest and a beer, I was back on the trail heading for Ponferrada.

Ponferrada gets its name from the iron bridge (Pons Ferrata) that exits the city. The area is known as an industrial hub built on coal and iron mining. The Los Templarios Castle has a moat and drawbridge, and houses the Knights Templar Library.

I met up with Rev. Gary from Wisconsin once again and we spent the afternoon together. There were some gnarly hills coming into the city. It's hard to describe how mentally draining it is when you've had a long, hot demanding walk and you discover that the steepest climb is at the very end.

Gary had a reservation at Albergue Guiana. This wasn't a typical municipal facility; it was a modern hotel calling itself an albergue. I hadn't booked anything, which had been my custom. I was feeling quite beat up as I approached the check-in counter. My heart sunk when I discovered that the very last bunk bed had just been taken. My sadness turned to euphoria when I found out that they had private rooms and there was one left. It was a steal at 25 Euros. I was overjoyed to have my own space and a private bathroom. Living with 50 or more people every night has that effect.

It was also a great opportunity to get my laundry done. The laundry room was state-of-the-art: ultramodern washers and dryers, drying racks with fans blowing hot air underneath and sinks with washboards. When I got there, both washing machines were in use. Pilgrims generally like to wash their clothes by hand and hang them to dry. I am a lazy pilgrim and chose the modern conveniences.

I was next in line and it wasn't too long before I put my clothes in the washer. I went back to my room and set the alarm on my phone. When I returned to put my clothes in the dryer, it was like Times Square in New York on a Friday night. It was utter bedlam. I think everyone on the Camino decided to do their laundry in this hotel, on this day. It was standing room only as people jockeyed to get in the queue.

I was slightly ahead of the curve and so didn't have to worry about my place in line. After putting five Euros in the dryer, I discovered that this particular brand of dryers actually didn't dry clothes. I hung them on a line and retrieved them several hours later.

I was sitting in the common room at the albergue finishing my journal when I noticed a young woman at the end of the table who was sitting alone and looking a bit forlorn. I introduced myself and had a lovely chat with Jin Park from South Korea. Not long after, my friend Klaus from Germany waltzed in, followed by my friend Lisa, also from Germany, who joined us. We decided to have dinner together.

We found a lovely restaurant in the massive plaza in the center of town and decided to sit outside. It was very quiet as we settled in for "tales from the Camino". The wine had barely been poured when the square started to fill. It was a cool and overcast night, so we were a bit puzzled at this sudden turn of events.

Before we could exchange a hello, all hell broke loose. There was a motorcade accompanied by loud music. The unmistakable sounds of Queen's *We Are the Champions* blared from many loudspeakers. Any attempted discussion was quickly drowned out. On a balcony above the square, several young, lithe soccer players appeared. The crowd went wild. This team must have won a game or a league championship. The crowd loved them.

We were eating dessert when the celebration ended. I hadn't learned much about my new friends, but vowed to interview them back at the albergue.

Hyunjin Park

Hyunjin, or Jin, is from Seoul, South Korea. She majored in business in university and has been a real estate investment specialist for five years, working with a company that deals in property acquisitions around the world. The work involves long hours and a lot of pressure.

The stress of the job caught up to her and she ended up sick. Why am I doing this? was a question Jin grappled with over and over again. As part of relaxation therapy, Jin embarked on courses leading to three certificates in yoga.

Jin loves travelling and every year in December, she thinks about her adventure goal for the next year. "On January 1st of this year, I went out for a long walk. I decided that this year I would walk and travel." In February, she went to the Himalayas and climbed to a height of 4,000 feet. While there, she thought about the Camino.

A promotion at work came with a mandatory 30-day vacation, which was the impetus for Jin to travel to Spain for the Camino. "I wanted to take a long walk to see if I could sort out a path going forward."

Like so many other walkers, Jin suffered injuries and was crippled by a bad leg for days on end. She received encouragement and support from newfound friends. "People you meet along the Camino are the highlight for me."

Camino Tip #17: Wear Sunscreen

This might seem painfully obvious, but in a country where sunshine seems ever-present, applying sunscreen early and often seems to be a prudent strategy. I saw many people with severe burns along the way. A corollary to this is to wear a wide-brimmed hat. Most pilgrims are walking anywhere from six to 10 hours per day and constant exposure to direct sunlight over three to four weeks could be quite harmful.

Chapter 18 – Ponferrada to Villafranca del Bierzo

25k/32,923 Steps

Today's walk took me through more of Spain's vast wine region. With the exception of the larger cities, the town of Cacabelos is one of the most modern looking on the Camino, despite a history that dates back to the 10th century. There is a wine museum and an archeological museum. One could spend years on the Camino just learning about the history of northern Spain. The small town of Villafranca del Bierzo–today's destination–like so many others along the way, relies heavily on the Camino. For a modest village, it has its share of churches and old monasteries. One of them, Iglesia de Santiago, has a special meaning for pilgrims. It is home to the Puerta del Perdón, the Door of Forgiveness. If you need a spiritual cleansing, you can get it at "the little Compostela".

With a relatively short walk ahead and having already booked my room in Villafranca del Bierzo, I decided to ease into the day. After breakfast, I wandered the streets looking for an ATM to replenish my cash supply (see Camino Tip #6). I had made arrangements the previous evening to interview my new friend from Germany, Lisa. We met in the lobby of the hotel and spent the next 90 minutes chatting. She is an intrepid global traveller and I was completely engaged in the discussion. It was only because she had to catch a lift to the next town that the interview didn't last longer.

I left the hotel at half past ten that morning, by far my latest departure time of the entire journey. It turned out to be a very hot day, with the temperature hitting the low 30s by noon. I stopped many times during the day.

I arrived at a café nestled in a glen before reaching Cacabelos. Despite my leisurely pace, the walk through thousands of acres of vineyards in the heat of the day was taking its toll, so finding this little oasis was a welcome sight.

La Siesta café is a small cabana set amid the shade of a copse. There was music from the 60s playing on loudspeakers suspended from the trees, and the tunes seemed to set the tone. Besides a few picnic tables, there were old leather sofas and chairs for a weary traveler to sit and relax. Over in a corner, next to a small river, was an enormous hammock. A family of four could easily share it. The signage, hung from another tree, was very artistic. The menu indicated that everything was organic.

Chatting with other pilgrims, I heard many fantastic reviews of the food here. Regrettably, I had eaten only a short time ago, but my lunch had not included dessert. The owner suggested a cookie with ice cream slathered in a homemade chocolate sauce. It was scrumptious, and I savoured every bite.

I could hear a commotion down by the river. I wondered if maybe someone had spotted a run of fish passing through. I hobbled over to discover several pilgrims sitting on the bank of the river with their feet submerged in the icy water. I immediately scrambled down the embankment and took off my shoes and my dust-filled socks. My feet were red and sore. The initial shock of the frigid water waned in seconds; it may have been one of the most soothing experiences of my life. I sat there in bliss for a full 10 minutes in the shade of the trees. In retrospect, I think this was the highlight of the entire walk. Finding such a unique spot in the middle of nowhere on a very hot day was a gift from the Camino that I will never forget.

I dried my feet and pulled on my footwear. Oddly, for the first time in recent memory, it didn't hurt to walk. It was then that I realized that my feet were numb from the icy water. The relief was short-lived, but psychologically it gave me a huge boost as I made my way toward Villafranca del Bierzo.

After climbing a rather steep incline, I could hear a commotion behind me. It was a group of cyclists. The cyclists were from Seattle, Washington State. The lead guy stopped to say a quick hello. This was his *eighteenth* Camino, all done by bike. I wondered what could possibly entice someone to cover the same ground over and over again. He said that he never gets tired of it and sees new things every time he comes over. Only upon completing the Camino did this make any sense to me. I dubbed the group "The Seattle Biker Gang". Oddly enough, I met up with them again later in the day. Obviously they travel faster than someone on foot, but there are places that require them to leave the trail and take a more circuitous route when passage on a bike is not possible.

I arrived at my destination of Albergue El Castillo late in the afternoon. This albergue had an enchanting back yard with lots of shade, tables and chairs. They also had a beer machine. As I rounded the corner of the building, I spotted a familiar face. Klaus Hubner from Germany was obviously moving at a similar pace to mine, although we hadn't actually walked together on the Camino. We did some laundry and had a few drinks. Later in the evening, we walked the streets of Villafranca del Bierzo. We didn't seek atonement at Iglesia de Santiago; our quest was simply to find the best paella in this beautiful small town. We shared a wonderful meal together getting caught up on our medical issues but mostly talking about our families. It was very obvious that he cared deeply about the folks back home.

I shared a room with about two dozen other pilgrims that night. I think the heat of the day had taken its toll on just about everyone, as silence enveloped the room much earlier than I had grown accustomed to.

Lisa K.

Lisa is originally from Flensburg, Germany, a town on the German-Danish border. Her ancestry includes Spanish, German and Danish.

Her work career has included careers in banking, travel and therapy. She has had a lifelong passion for traveling and has seen a lot of the world. She would like to become a spiritual writer.

The following poem, written by Lisa, sums up nicely the experience she has gleaned as a globetrotter:

Hello beautiful!
Dance in the rain
Make love in the ocean
Sing in the forest
Cry under a tree
Kiss the sun hello
Embrace the stars
Honour your lovers
Smile at strangers
Hug the children
Bow to your neighbours
Ride the clouds
Bless the flowers
Surrender to your desires
Fall in love again and again
Celebrate, celebrate and celebrate every minute, hour and day...
and always remember, you are love and perfect
just the way you are!!!

Written by Lisa K. Germany in 2015

Camino Tip #18: Ice Your Feet at the End of the Day

I had an "Aha!" moment on the Camino that day. As a former marathon runner, I knew about the healing power of ice baths after completing a 42.2k run. Plunging my feet into frigid water had given me enormous, albeit short-lived relief. Most albergues don't have ice readily available but they do have cold water. At the end of every day when taking a shower, turn off the hot water for a few minutes and direct the showerhead towards your feet—they will love you for it.

Chapter 19 –Villafranca del Bierzo to O Cebreiro

29k/42,720 Steps

If you like mountains, long climbs and stunning vistas, the walk from Villafranca del Bierzo to O Cebreiro provides all of this and more. The small village of O Cebreiro is located in Galicia, just over the border from the Castilla y León region. It sits on a high ridge facing the mountains. The village is filled with ancient roundhouses and cobbled streets. It is the site of the Miracle of the Eucharist. Apparently, back in the 12th century, a poor peasant and very devout Catholic braved his way through a vicious storm to attend mass. The priest made fun of the peasant for traveling so far to receive bread and wine. Legend has it that the bread and wine were turned into flesh and blood.

The Iglesia de Santa María Real is one of the oldest churches associated with the Camino, dating back to the ninth century. The church is where Don Elias Valiňa Samperdo is buried. He worked tirelessly in the 1900s to restore and preserve the integrity of the Camino. The yellow waymarks that dot the Camino were his idea. The modern version of the Camino owes much to this man.

After a good night's sleep (a relative term), I was out the door at six o'clock, my favourite time of day. I loved walking through small villages in the wee hours of the morning before they came to life. However, as I have discovered, many of these places are virtually abandoned and it seems like the Camino is the only game in town. I rarely, if ever, saw young children playing in the streets. It seems that every village has a dog or two. They are obviously used to seeing walkers, because they rarely move from a sleeping position as you pass.

The first 20 kilometres were pretty bland, as the trail here runs alongside a major highway. I stopped in a small town where I decided to grab a bite before the nine-kilometre climb ahead of me. I entered a darkened café to discover that the power was out all over town, which meant no coffee, no fresh-squeezed orange juice and (gasp) no croissants. I had to settle for homemade apple cake and bottled orange juice.

The passage leaving the town pointed directly uphill. The first three kilometres were easy enough, as the path was wide and well groomed. It quickly deteriorated into an all-too-common goat trail. I embraced the challenge; walking steep hills is more about attitude than altitude. At least, that's what I kept telling myself! There were a lot of people struggling mightily to make the ascent.

Sweating profusely, I stopped in a small village. There were a dozen or so pilgrims catching their breath before the next challenge. There was an outdoor fountain with ice cold water running through the taps. I doused myself, had a beer and made my way back onto the trail. The next leg was no less challenging than the first, but the Camino always rewards effort. Coming around a turn, I was greeted by jaw-dropping scenery. It reminded me of the opening scene of The Sound of Music. I half expected to see Julie Andrews and the Von Trapp family come marching over the mountain. For the remainder of that day's walk, I sang every song from this classic musical.

I paused several times to take pictures of the views. I also took some for other pilgrims and had my own photo taken. On one of these photo shoots, I managed to put my sunglasses on the ground. I discovered later in the day that they were no longer perched on my Tilley hat. So far, I had lost my phone charger, my soap and now my sunglasses. At this rate, my backpack was going to be empty by the time I arrived at my destination.

I met up with Charlotte Jones, a massage therapist from Dallas, Texas. We walked together for the rest of the day. When you encounter a herd of cows on the Camino, you yield to them. They have the right of way. Watching a herdsman and his dog keep order is a special thing. Charlotte and I stood patiently on the side of the road to let a herd pass and then followed them dutifully into the next village. With several other pilgrims walking with us, it was an odd-looking parade, and several people in the village were taking photos and videos of the procession.

Charlotte received a distressing call during our walk. I watched as her face turned pale. It was, as I expected, a death in the family. Two, actually. Charlotte was the owner of three chickens, and two of them had inexplicably passed away. My immediate thought was that desertion by their owner was the cause of death. Apparently, the third chicken is in therapy!

We arrived in O Cebreiro early that afternoon. Charlotte was moving on to the next town, so we shared a beverage and she was on her way.

My accommodations that night were first class. I had booked a private room at Casa Carola. At 40 Euros, it was a bit pricey, but treating oneself from time to time is well worth it. My room had two beds, and I felt a bit ashamed to have this luxury in a very busy village where rooms were hard to come by. I decided that I would offer the second bed to a fellow walker in need.

After getting cleaned up I strolled through town, soaking up the sun and the incredible scenery. I spotted someone that I had met briefly a few days earlier. Maria Gustafsson from Sweden was in obvious pain. I asked her where she was staying for the night. She said that she hoped to find a bed in one of the albergues, but the word was out that there were no rooms left anywhere. She was pondering going to the next town some five kilometres away. I made the offer of a place to stay. I showed her my room and before she even said yes, her backpack had been tossed in the corner. While this type of arrangement might seem odd in the real world, on the Camino it is perfectly normal.

Not surprisingly at this altitude, the wifi was spotty or nonexistent. For some people this was stressful, but being detached from the rest of the world definitely has its own rewards—like serenity.

Maria Gustafsson

Maria is from Sweden. She manages an office for social workers. She got married at an early age and quickly had two children. When the children were ages one and two, her husband left her. Not long after, both of her parents died. Life was not easy as a single mother.

When the children were still young, she developed debilitating back problems. She spent six months in bed with excruciating pain. She walked with the aid of a cane for nearly four years. It took years of therapy before she was able to truly get back on her feet.

Maria came to the Camino trying to answer three questions: Would her new relationship work? Where would she decide to live: in Norway near her daughter and grandchildren, or in Sweden near her son? Was it time to change careers?

*Regarding the latter, she admits to loving her job
but not the company culture. "I don't fit in.
Maybe if I had the same job with a different
company, I would be happier."*

*As for her Camino experience, so far she had
effusive praise for fellow pilgrims. "People are so
open-minded and kind to each other. It is like a
travelling family. At the beginning of the journey,
there is a fascination for what lies ahead, but you
become more introspective as the days go by.
People become physically tired and mentally
fatigued as they try to process things."*

*Sadly, a few days after doing this interview,
Maria's injuries became so serious that a doctor
recommended she immediately stop walking.*

Camino Tip #18 – Exhibit Positive Body Language

Nobody who walks 700-800 kilometres finds it particularly easy. Most pilgrims learn to cope with discomfort, which comes in many varieties. Body language says a lot about a person. If you look downtrodden and beaten up, you probably are. This is not to dismiss the very real pain and struggles of doing an epic walk, but looking positive and walking with purpose, when possible, can turn a bad day into something very gratifying.

Chapter 20 – O Cebreiro to Fontearcuda

28K/42,955 Steps

Today's walk was a bit like a roller coaster ride. The path from O Cebreiro to Triacastela is primarily downhill and hard on the quads. Once you leave Triacastela the way is mainly a series of ups and downs. Be well rested if you happen to take this route. Triacastela, as the name suggests, was the town of three castles and was an important stop for pilgrims coming from a long walk through the mountains. It is believed that Norman invaders in 968 AD destroyed the castles. A pilgrim needs to pay attention when they reach Triacastela because there are two distinct routes to get to Sarria. The northern route is via San Xil and the southern route via Samos. The southern route travels near a major highway and is over six kilometres longer.

I left O Cebreiro early with no fixed destination and was greeted by a stunning sunrise. Very often in the mountains, the rolling mist creates an optical illusion that reveals the hills to be seemingly hanging above the clouds. I had checked my guidebook the night before and was quite surprised that the first hour of the day was still uphill.

I caught up to Charlotte from Texas once again mid-morning, and we would spend the rest of the day together. We had lunch in Triacastela and I asked about the mental state of Blanche, the surviving chicken! Despite the challenging terrain we had faced all morning, we both felt it was too early in the day to stop and opted to move on towards Sarria on the northern route through San Xil. It started to rain as we departed and we were faced with a formidable hill to start our afternoon. A short time later, we met up with a cyclist. The terrain was very rugged and she didn't have a map. We showed her the alternate route and it didn't take her long to backtrack and head south.

In many ways, this was probably the most physically challenging day for both of us. Our feet were sore and our muscles ached from the constant change in altitude with severe climbs and steep descents. We checked our maps and realized that we had very few options for a place to stay that night.

After passing through the tiny village of Montán, we crested a hill and spied an old run down barn, which didn't appear to have any doors. We could hear music, laughter, and chatter. It looked like something right out of the 1960s. I immediately dubbed it "the hippie farm". There was all manner of furniture inside the main structure, much of it appearing to have been there for decades. Like many other pop-up relief stations, the hippie farm also had food and drink available on a table including fruit, dates, nuts, cookies, tea and coffee. You could take what you wanted with the expectation of a donation in return. I spotted two guitars in the corner of the barn.

An older guy appeared to be the head hippie. He told us that some people come here and stay overnight while others stay longer, sometimes for weeks at a time. There were a few other dilapidated buildings on the premises with no running water or electricity. Pilgrims were welcome to stay. We inquired about other possible local accommodations, knowing the next town was five kilometres away. We were in no shape to walk anymore.

The head hippie said that there was a private home about eight hundred metres up the road. Neither Charlotte nor I were much interested in being life members of the commune, nor overnight guests.

After some sustenance, we strapped on our backpacks and trudged along the trail. I jokingly said to Charlotte that maybe this place could turn out to be a small jewel. How prophetic! We found the sign for Casa do Campo and stared in disbelief, as the road leading to this home was by far the steepest either of us had encountered on the Camino. Our quads were already fried; the descent was painful.

"The Camino gives you what you need, not what you want."

At this moment, we desperately needed a place to stay for the night. The farm was nestled in an idyllic setting. There were several barns and a large stone house. They also had a café in a separate small stone building. The owner met us after her two dogs announced our arrival. She took us inside and showed us around. I would have happily slept in one of the barns at this juncture.

The family lived on the main floor and there were four guest rooms upstairs. The whole place was spectacular. In the upstairs hallway there was a floor-to-ceiling library. The rooms were large and a few of them afforded beautiful rural scenery. They were beautifully appointed, but the piece de resistance was the shared bathroom. It was very spacious and immaculately clean. And it had a Jacuzzi!

For all of this luxury, we were offered a room for twelve Euros. We thought we had died and gone to heaven. After getting cleaned up, we went next door to the café and sat on the back patio. We were shaded from the sun by large trees while birds chirped merrily. We both agreed that this was the best find on the Camino as far as lodgings went.

Supper was stupendous. A gourmet pasta was followed by a hot vegetable dish which included broccoli, green beans, mushrooms and more. There was plenty of warm homemade bread and red wine. The ice cream for dessert was fabulous. Even if the meal had been ordinary, when you've had a very difficult day of walking and you find a private spa, everything seems right with the world.

112

I was far too tired to get into the Jacuzzi after dinner—I feared falling asleep and drowning in a whirlpool!

I was stiff, sore and very happy climbing into bed. I decided to read a bit of my new book about *Don Quixote* but sleep overtook me.

Charlotte Jones

Charlotte was born in Waco, Texas but has lived in the Dallas area since 1982. She has worked as a licensed massage therapist since 1994.

The notion of doing the Camino came from a Facebook post in 2018. A woman in a group that Charlotte belonged to had done the Camino and when she saw a photo of her friend with her backpack at the airport, her interest was piqued.

The loss of her brother in 2002, compounded by a difficult stretch in her life from 2013 to 2018, prompted her to tackle the Camino. "I felt like the universe reached out, gave me a shake and said 'you need to do this.' In actuality, the universe said, 'you are going to do this.' "

Several things ran through Charlotte's mind. She had never taken that much time off work and she had never traveled alone to a foreign country. Her mother had some misgivings and wondered if her daughter had lost her sanity! "I realized that I can't prevent others from worrying about me."

Charlotte faced her fears head on. "I learned to listen to and trust my body." She may have been one of the only people not to suffer the scourge of blisters while walking the Camino. While many people see the Camino as a spiritual pilgrimage, Charlotte had misgivings about organized religion before coming to Spain, which only seemed to be reinforced by her long trek across the country. "I reconfirmed that my church was now in the forests."

She loved the solitude of walking through farm land and vineyards. Even the smell of manure was comforting; it reminded her of home.

"I'm still processing and unpacking the whole experience. I discovered that the grief of the past several years, that I thought I was handling well, was not being handled very well at all."

Like so many pilgrims, her encounters with people from far-flung countries were a rich experience.

Camino Tip #20: Take the Road Less Travelled

There are many opportunities in life to choose alternate paths, and the Camino also provides these in abundance. Today was a great example. Many pilgrims choose the southern route, which is somewhat longer but much less arduous. I can't imagine not having had the chance to see the "hippie farm" and find the best accommodations on the Camino. Dare to be different.

114

Chapter 21 – Fontearcuda

Rest Day

I woke before dawn today and listened to the birds.

Having discovered this small treasure along the Camino in the remotest of locations, I had decided to stay an extra day. I was on no fixed schedule and my body was telling me that a rest day was required. I was also aware that several of my friends were a day or two behind me, so it made perfect sense to stay put and relax.

Charlotte and I had a simple breakfast. I told her my plans, but she was determined to forge on. I walked her back up the steep incline until it connected with the trail. We bade each other farewell and that is the last I saw of her. I watched her disappear over a hill and I returned to "the spa".

When I'd been lying in bed earlier that morning trying to decide on my plan for the day, the number one reason for staying had been the Jacuzzi. Spending another day here afforded me the luxury of having a relaxing soak without worrying about tying up the bathroom. When you're on the road, you're always conscious of other pilgrims and their needs. Taking long, hot showers in albergues is frowned upon, because everyone deserves a bit of hot water at the end of a long day of walking.

I must admit that I can't ever remember being in a private Jacuzzi. I have been in several outdoor hot tubs and the ones they have in hotels, but never in a bathroom. Every muscle in my body ached from the wear and tear of nearly three weeks of walking, combined with yesterday's travails. The sides of the tub were so high that I wondered if I would be able to get my legs to cooperate. I turned on the hot water and put my head back. It was rapturous even before turning on the jets. My entire body—particularly my feet—were deliriously happy.

It took quite a while for the tub to fill; this was a beast and required a lot of water. I watched carefully as the levels rose to cover the half dozen jets, and I hit the start button. It didn't make the smooth, soothing sound I had expected. Rather, it sounded more like an angry bull that had been poked with a cattle prod. There was an explosion of water and, despite the fact that this was a very large bathroom, the spray seemed to find its way to all four walls, the floor and the toilet. Let's not forget the ceiling, as water now surrounded me and even dripped from above. I turned the jets to the *off* position. I wasn't sure what to do next.

I concluded that there hadn't been enough water in the tub and now there was even less, as half of it adorned every square inch of the bathroom. I stepped out and turned on the hot water tap again. I grabbed my bath towel, which was only moderately wet, and started wiping down the entire bathroom. I prayed that there wasn't a secret camera taping this entire escapade. I was terrified of falling, but not because of the possibility of broken bones. No, I was worried that I might not be able to get up off the floor and someone would eventually discover me sprawled in the midst of the large mess I'd made.

I re-entered the Jacuzzi, which now contained enough water to float an ocean liner. I gingerly turned on the jets again and could hear a low thrum. I was in business. The jets blasted water at every square inch of my body. Every sinew, muscle, ligament, tendon, organ and extremity sang the *Hallelujah* chorus. There was even a jet at the back of my neck, a perpetual thorn in my side (neck!). After about 25 minutes of luxuriating I pulled the plug, fearing death by relaxation.

I dried myself off with a wet towel.

116

I lay on my bed for a while reading about *Don Quixote*. I had a snooze and woke feeling like a million dollars. I was so enthralled with the hippie farm from the previous day that I decided to wander back and give it a closer look. Of course, I was walking the opposite way on the Camino and I got some odd looks from pilgrims. I saw several people that I knew.

The farm was buzzing with activity. There were 30 or so pilgrims resting and snacking. It was a beautiful morning and there was a very positive vibe in the air. I saw familiar faces: Lily (Russia), Aleksandra and Magdalena (Poland) and two women from Sweden that I'd passed several days ago.

I went over to chat with the head hippie. Luis has been a mainstay of this place for several years. He has done the Camino many times and has spent long stretches of time as the de facto leader of this fascinating place. Apparently, some foreigners actually own the property but it runs entirely independently. With the donations they collect for food and drink, they go to the nearest town and buy more goods. The whole operation is self-financing. Of course, they're not paying for water, sewer or electrical so one suspects it's a low cost enterprise.

I asked Luis if I could play one of the guitars and he was happy to oblige. He grabbed the other one and he was an excellent player, able to pick while I strummed chords. It seems everyone in the universe knows John Denver's *Country Roads*. The music drew a crowd and there were lots of pictures taken and videos recorded. Luis asked me for an Irish tune and when I started playing *The Gypsy Rover*, he grabbed a marionette, which proceeded to dance to the immense joy of the crowd. Music remains my constant companion when I'm traveling.

I chatted with my Camino friends and headed back to the spa for a light lunch. Earlier that morning, using hand signals, I had been able to convey to the owner my desire for some lunch at noon. My typical lunch has been a sandwich and a beer, but today she opened a fresh bottle of red wine as I sat down at the table. It was 12:01, and I quickly determined that any drinking after noon hour was acceptable!

She presented me with a plate heaped with luscious pieces of fresh fish, which looked and tasted like halibut. There was a side plate of boiled potatoes, homemade bread and salad. I hadn't had the opportunity to enjoy many salads on this trip and I'm certain that the bowl of greens, tomatoes and onions straight from their garden physically left me drooling, it was that tasty. As hard as it is to believe, I turned down dessert. There was simply no room left in my stomach. The cost of this "light lunch" was seven Euros.

As I was heading back to my room, the owner presented me with the laundry she'd graciously agreed to wash for me. I'd seen it fluttering on the line earlier, and it was hard to imagine that socks, underwear and t-shirts could smell this fresh. She asked for three Euros; after my recent less than ideal experiences with laundry, I felt this was a great bargain.

I collapsed on my bed from the weight of the food and slept again.

I received a message from Jan (Germany). He was still not feeling 100%. When I told him about my current living arrangements, he asked me to book a room for him. I went up to the trail a few hours later to meet him. He couldn't keep the grin off his face when he saw his surroundings for the next 12 hours.

We retreated to the café late that afternoon to grab a cold brew. Two chaps from Spain were sitting at one of the two tables in the café. We said hello, grabbed our beer and went out on the back patio, inviting Luis and Isaac to join us. There was instant chemistry, and these may have been three of the funniest guys that I've met. Luis and Isaac had started off by warning us that their humour was very dark, and they didn't disappoint. Many well-intentioned insults

118

filled the air. I asked Isaac if he was offended by some of our commentary on his poetry. "You would have to be born two or three more times and spit in my face rude words about my family in a civilized language like Latin to offend me."

Luis was ranting about Instagram and how tiresome he finds it watching people post food pictures, especially meals. He showed me his Instagram account. He displays dirty plates with just the remnants of the meal visible on the plate, leaving his followers to wonder what he had just eaten. They also told us that Spanish people learn foreign languages by simply raising their voices several decibels! I won't tell you how many drinks and how many hours later we wound up the conversation, but I have never laughed so loud or so long in my life.

We were served another fantastic meal. You can cue the broken record, but this was certainly *the* best 48 hours of my Camino. My body and mind were both well rested; an evening of friendship and laughter was the best medicine anyone could prescribe.

I went to bed with a huge grin on my face.

Camino Tip #21: Whenever and Wherever Possible, Sing

Music is the universal language, and nowhere is this more apparent than on the Camino. There is rarely a day when someone isn't belting out a song from their home country. There's something very therapeutic about singing, especially in the outdoors. So, go ahead and do your best Pavarotti imitation, especially when you're alone. The sheep and cows aren't too critical.

Chapter 22 – Fontearcuda to Portomarín

31k/50,784 Steps

Today's walk brought me through the city of Sarria. It has become a major starting point for pilgrims who don't have time to do the entire Camino. People who start at Sarria can still get their Compostela, which is the official certificate indicating completion of the Camino. The trail takes on a decidedly different feel, as the crowds are much larger. Many of these walkers are tourists and will have their bags taken from one stage to the next and stay in nice hotels, which I personally believe takes away some of the authenticity of the walk. There are more accommodations from Sarria to Santiago de Compostela but they fill up quickly. If you're not the spontaneous type, booking ahead for the last 110k might be a good idea.

Many photos are taken outside the city of Sarria, where the large stone waymark signifies 100 kilometres remaining to get to Santiago de Compostela.

Portomarín is yet another town rich with history, much of it related to the earliest pilgrimages. Prominent among the local architecture are old slate houses and traditional wine cellars very common in this wine-producing region. Portomarín is one of the towns also known for producing spirits. Make no mistake, wine is king in Spain, but the country also produces spirits from local plants, such as anise, as well as some more common drinks, such as brandy and rum.

I hated to leave Fontearcuda and my newfound oasis of tranquility. Nonetheless, I was on the go bright and early on a sun-dappled morning. I arrived in Sarria around eight o'clock. After breakfast, I went in search of a bank machine. Sarria is a fairly big town and it took quite a while for me to find one. As I approached the ATM, I looked across the street and noticed a familiar figure. It was Maria Gustafsson. It's amazing when you bump into people you know in obscure places on the Camino. Maria had spoken to a doctor, who had told her that she might do irreparable harm to her leg if she continued to walk. She had wisely decided to heed the advice and was now travelling from town to town by bus, doing the tourist thing.

I had to find my way back to the trail, so Maria walked with me. We approached a bridge crossing the Rio Sarria and we ran into none other than Jan. We would spend the rest of the day walking together to Portomarín.

As we made our way through the town and reached the countryside, the entire feel of the Camino changed instantly. I had rarely seen more than a half dozen walkers together at one time in the last three weeks. Now the trail was crowded with hundreds of new pilgrims just beginning their Camino. Many of them, sporting nametags, were obviously from a tour group.

There were busloads of school children being dropped off. It appeared that they were going for an "end of school year" nature walk.

By reason of sheer numbers, it could be argued that the most photographed place on the entire Camino, even more than Cruz de Ferro, is the stone waymark in Sarria. Not surprisingly, there were lineups to have one's picture taken in front of this monument. Jan and I were not among those waiting for this precious photo. There was another marker just a kilometre just down the road, indicating 99 kilometres to Santiago. We chose this one for our photo op!

I come from a part of the world (Nova Scotia, Canada) where the "skirl of the pipes" is quite common. Bagpipes are very popular among those who have Scottish roots. You can imagine my total surprise when just a few hundred metres after the 99K marker, I could hear the familiar strains of the pipes. I wondered if I was suffering from heatstroke but sure enough, in a small glen with a river behind it, stood a bagpiper playing his heart out. The Highland Fling is a very popular dance performed by the Scots. It wasn't easy, but I did my Scottish duty and performed a few steps of the Fling with my backpack on my back. The piper seemed amused. Of course, I dropped a few Euros into his open bagpipe carrying case.

Unlike the previous weeks, I knew the last days of my Camino would be a challenge. This was evident at the first café we came upon after leaving Sarria. There were lineups for food and lineups for the bathroom. The place was noisy and felt more like a bar in a big city on a Saturday night.

Despite the heavy traffic, the trail was quite scenic. The first 15 kilometres were mostly uphill and the second were mostly downhill. We bumped into Jin, who was still struggling but absolutely determined to finish the journey.

I also met, for the first time, Virginie Gatel, an athletic woman from Britanny, France. She walked with Jan and me for about 20 minutes before going off on her own.

It was a long haul, and the last few kilometers proved to be the most difficult of the day. At the outskirts of the city there were two yellow arrows pointing in different directions, both leading into the town. I had met a father and son from Singapore earlier that week and today, at this intersection, I met them again as they were now joined by the wife and daughter of the man. They went one way and we went the other. We were lucky to have traversed many difficult paths before now, because our route into Portomarín was exceedingly difficult. The path was very narrow, steep and uneven, even for seasoned veterans. Each step had to be chosen carefully.

We crossed a long bridge into Portomarín. I was tired and hot and slightly annoyed by the onslaught on the Camino today. We decided to check the municipal albergue first. It was very bland and didn't have a great vibe. For only the second time on the Camino, I had found an albergue with no blankets. As we were being escorted to our dorm, a couple was being asked to relocate to another room that wasn't quite full, even though they had been told that they could pick any bed in the facility. I told Jan that I was going to see if there was anything else available in town.

The second place I visited was full, but a helpful desk clerk called a different hostel for me. I was handed the phone and the person on the other end offered me a private room. It was only a short walk to this hotel but when I got there, the owners, an elderly couple, appeared puzzled. We didn't speak each other's language and I tried in vain to explain that I had been promised a room. We reached an impasse–I eventually gave up and continued my search, to no avail.

Somewhat disconsolately, I trudged back to the municipal albergue. I reckoned I had walked an extra three kilometres trying to find a bed for the night. I resigned myself to this less than satisfactory hostel, but one quickly gets over these minor irritations on the Camino.

After showering, we headed into town for supper. The main street had dozens of food establishments and the outdoor patios were jam-packed. This lifted our spirits, as did the giant glass of beer we consumed on the patio before the sun dipped behind a giant cathedral across the street. Shortly thereafter we noticed Klaus sitting at a corner table. Virginie had showed up earlier as well, so the four of us dined together, agreeing that the paella we had just consumed was the best we'd had.

With full bellies, spirited conversation and a glass or two of red wine, the albergue looked better as we headed home to bed.

Luis Trullenque

Luis is from Zaragoza, Spain, but has spent a good portion of his working life abroad in Switzerland and the UK in the banking industry. For the past three years he has worked as a consultant, and he recently moved back to Spain.

Due to time constraints, Luis has had to do the Camino in stages, beginning in 2014. It has taken him five years to complete his journey, which he accomplished this year. "My primary reasons for doing the Camino were religious and spiritual. I felt I need some space and time to think about things."

He enjoyed all aspects of the walk, including the history, the scenery, the food and, of course, the people he met along the trail.

Luis says that the experience was one of mindfulness. "The Camino presented me with the opportunity to hit the reset button and to have the time to spend with old friends, getting caught up. It allowed me to gain new perspectives on my life."

Camino Tip #22: Book Ahead From Sarria to Santiago

Sarria presents the pilgrim with a new set of variables: while there are more accommodations on the last hundred kilometres of the Camino, the crowds are much bigger, and getting a place to sleep is not guaranteed. While booking ahead takes some of the spontaneity out of things, at this point in the journey it is just the reality. After 600 kilometres of walking, making sure you have a place to stay is rather important.

Chapter 23 – Portomarín to Melide

41k/59,297 Steps

The first several kilometres out of Portomarín are heavily forested and quite beautiful. It's good to be aware that the first available café is in the village of Gonzar. As you enter Gonzar, you will find two waymarks pointing in different directions. One path takes you into the village, while the other stays close to the highway. Melide is a fairly large town, with many of the bars and restaurants serving a regional specialty, Pulpo Gallego. This popular tapas dish is served throughout the region of Galicia, where octopus is a common catch for local fishermen.

Never judge a book by its cover. This would be an apt description of the place I'd stayed the previous night. There were only a handful of pilgrims scattered throughout the large room where I slept. Nobody snored, which by now you'll understand is pretty amazing, and there were no waits for washroom or shower facilities. Despite not being provided with a blanket, I'd slept well in the comfortable temperature of the dorm.

My phone battery was perilously low as I prepared to start my day, but thankfully I knew where to get my phone charged; they'd had an outdoor electrical outlet with an extension cord at the restaurant where we'd dined the previous night. Brilliant, if you ask me! I was also able to access the internet while waiting for the battery to replenish.

It was overcast and foggy as I exited the town and crossed a bridge leading into the forest. I stopped momentarily to turn on my phone flashlight, as it was pitch black in the woods, and I could hear footsteps coming from behind. Lily from Russia seems to be a ubiquitous presence on the Camino. She was in full flight and didn't stop to talk. My first goal that day was to meet up with Aleksandra and Magdalena in Gonzar, just under nine kilometres away.

When I reached the two waymarks on the outskirts of Gonzar. I could see the village to my left. My instincts told me to go this way, which turned out to be a mistake. I entered the sleepy village but could not find our chosen meeting place. Granted, Gonzar isn't downtown Paris, but when you don't know where you're going, you don't have internet service and you don't speak Spanish, this can be problematic. I found a woman who used hand gestures to point me in the right direction. I wandered aimlessly for another full 30 minutes before finally meeting two walkers on the trail two kilometers from Gonzar. They set me straight and a short time later I reached my destination. I later discovered that had I used the other waymark, I would have arrived in fewer than five minutes.

I had my breakfast and reconnected with my two Polish friends, as well as Maty from Argentina. I sang a rousing version of *O Canada* before we headed out. Jan showed up just as we arrived on the trail and the five of us formed a small army. The energy level was high, as were our spirits. It was the perfect start to a very long day–the longest of my Camino–ahead of me. As we were grinding out the kilometers, I decided to lighten things up even further by singing *The Happy Wanderer* in its entirety, which seemed appropriate. When I finished, my two Polish friends sang a rollicking, high spirited tune from their home country. Maty sang a passionate song from Argentina, a country he hadn't seen in seven years. Not to be outdone, Jan rounded things out with a well-known German song.

Someone suggested that we sing a song we all knew. I reckoned that *Happy Birthday* might fill the bill. There was dancing and laughter as we proceeded arm and arm along the path. When we finished, Jan seemed a bit emotional. It just so happened that today was his birthday, which coincided with the anniversary of the death of his father a few years back.

We stopped for lunch in a town that was obviously hosting a soccer tournament. The restaurant we chose was packed with young athletes in uniform. The place was absolute madness. Unbeknownst to all of us, Maty managed to talk to a staff person and part way through our meal, they brought over a small cupcake with a candle and we sang *Happy Birthday* for the second time that day.

Later that afternoon during another café stop, we met up with Felicity and Virginie. Everyone seemed to be feeling a similar sense of dread, knowing that our Camino was rapidly drawing to a close. Aleksandra and Magdalena encouraged us to continue on to Melide, which would push our walk that day to 41 kilometres. We had already walked 25 and were feeling it. It had become quite warm, but we decided to push onward. By the time we reached Melide later in the day, we were fried and Jan was feeling very unwell.

We checked into the Xaneiro Hotel. Our room was one floor up from the lobby. The elevator seemed to have been designed for tiny people from a different galaxy. There was no way two medium-sized adults could fit, let alone with backpacks. Actually, it wasn't possible for one person with a backpack to fit. We returned to the front desk to ask about the availability of beer. Armed with fortifications, we were able to make it up the stairwell.

We cleaned up and had a rest before going back down to dinner. Jan took a few bites of his meal, determined he was not up for eating and retreated to the bedroom. I was one of the last diners and decided to use the time to write in my journal.

Sleep came easily that night.

Isaac Clemente

Isaac is from Cáceres, on the western side of Spain, near the border of Portugal. He was a banker for 10 years but for the last three he has been a management consultant.

Besides his day job, Isaac was an active poet from 1995 to 2009, reaching the final stages of some poetry competitions.

This is not Isaac's first Camino. The previous two times, he did it on a bicycle. His friend Luis asked him to walk with him this year. "I just jumped in when Luis asked me to go with him. Walking the Camino is much more intense than doing it on a bicycle. You have more time to appreciate the details."

"I have been writing poetry for years and recently have been learning how to write narrative." He quit his job a year ago and has been working on a book. He has been studying and practicing the technique of writing a novel for a year. This includes long form writing, short form writing, reading theory and a lot of narrative. He hopes to begin writing his novel in the fall of 2019.

"A long walk on the Camino seemed like a good opportunity to take a break and gain some introspection."

*Besides having lots of time to think and reflect,
Isaac enjoyed the opportunity to spend time in
nature. He also enjoyed the food and the people.
Having a good sense of humour, he also had plenty
of laughs.*

Camino Tip # 23: Take Short Showers

A shower of any description on the Camino is welcome. Most people are accustomed to a steaming shower in their daily lives but in many of the albergues, hot water is in short supply. Being respectful of fellow pilgrims is an unwritten code, so when taking a shower, keep it brief. You know how it feels when someone stays in too long and you're the one who ends up in the cold.

Chapter 24 – Melide to Salceda de Caselas

28k/42,051 Steps

The trail passes through the town of Arzúa, which is the only town where two Camino routes meet. The Camino Primitivo (Original Way) stops in Arzúa and the Camino Francés (French Way) passes through. Due to the two routes meeting in this town, it is well equipped and accustomed to helping pilgrims. Arzúa is known for its local cheese and the cheese fair held there in March each year.

It was hard to believe that my Camino would end the following day. I was looking forward to resting my feet but was dreading the end of this remarkable journey.

I hadn't quite finished my journaling the night before, so early in the morning I went down to the hotel lobby to complete the task. A sign indicated that there wouldn't be anybody at the front desk until eight o'clock, and the lobby was shrouded in darkness. I fumbled around, looking for a light switch. None was to be found, however I discovered that the lights were activated by motion. I'm sure the security camera footage would have been hilarious, with me flailing my arms literally every 60 seconds to keep the lights on while I wrote.

It also dawned on me when I woke up that morning that we hadn't paid for our dinner last evening. Jan had left the table mid-meal and I'd simply gotten up after eating and waltzed off to my room. With no one at the front desk, I needed to find someone to pay. I entered the small café attached to the hotel lobby. An older couple stood behind the counter. I discovered that they were involved in all aspects of the hotel, including the dining room. I confessed my sin of omission, and the woman behind the counter gave me a warm smile. "We noticed that last night but weren't worried. We knew you would come by to pay."

Jan skipped breakfast, as he was still feeling quite ill. We left at eight and made our way out of Melide. Early in our walk, we met up once again with Virginie, and she and I would spend the remainder of the day together. It was a beautiful walk through eucalyptus-lined paths.

When we reached Arzúa, Jan decided that he couldn't go any further and got himself a hotel room. Our Polish friends had left Meilde later than us and asked us to wait for them here. Virginie and I had a long, leisurely lunch. We waited for more than an hour before our friends caught up to us. They, in turn, were waiting for friends behind them. Virginie was quite fatigued from yesterday's walk and was trying to decide whether to stay in Arzúa or to move on. I determined that I was not going to delay any further, and she ultimately decided to continue on with me.

We did a lot of singing along the way. I was surprised at her awareness of older music. *Let it Be* and *We Are the Champions* were her favourites. She especially liked the line "no time for losers" from *We Are the Champions*. This refrain was repeated dozens of times over the next two days.

We were both very tired late in the afternoon and decided to stay in the small village of Salceda de Caselas. There were only three choices of lodging, all within walking distance of one another. The first one we came to had rooms available but no other amenities. We declined and went to check out the other two, which were both completely full. We marched back to the first place and were distraught to discover that in the space of 15 minutes, all the rooms had been booked. The next town was five kilometres away, and the thought of more walking was unpalatable to both of us.

Virginie checked her guidebook, which wasn't the same one I was using. She discovered that there was a small pension (hotel) one kilometre away, just off of the trail. Luckily, with her ability to speak Spanish, she was able to call ahead and reserve a room.

We were thoroughly whipped as we got to the hotel and registered. We had a great dinner and did some laundry before calling it a day.

I reflected on the day before falling asleep. Once again, as has happened so many times in my life, music had been a big part of my day. I was walking with someone who didn't share the same language. With limited knowledge of each other's mother tongue, we still managed to understand each other perfectly well. It was when we started singing songs together that we really felt connected. Music brings people together. While some music can be mournful and sad, singing well-known songs often results in smiles and laughter. Virginie and I laughed and sang our way across the Galician countryside.

Camino Tip # 24: Celebrate Your Good Fortune

You're healthy. You have the time. You have the financial resources to travel. Being able to walk the Camino is a great privilege. Many people simply aren't able to do this. Being consciously grateful is very important and nowhere is this more apparent than on a pilgrimage like this. Pilgrims should acknowledge that they are among the privileged, given this rare chance to do something unique and powerful.

Chapter 25 – Salceda de Caselas to Santiago de Compostela

29k/43,089 Steps

This is the home stretch and arguably the busiest portion of the entire Camino. Many pilgrims will spend their penultimate day a few kilometres outside of Santiago so that they can walk their final day and arrive in time for the pilgrim mass at noon. Santiago is the capital of northwest Spain's Galicia region. It is known as the culmination of all Camino de Santiago pilgrimage routes and the burial site of the Biblical apostle St. James. His remains rest in the Catedral de Santiago de Compostela.

The pilgrim mass is one of the highlights of the Camino. The Catedral contains possibly the largest censers in the world. A censer is a container in which incense is burned, typically during a religious ceremony. The Botafumeiro, or smoke expeller, is the famous censer in this church. It weighs fifty-three kilograms and measures over five feet tall. It sits suspended 20 metres above the cathedral floor. On special occasions or after certain masses, a group of eight tiraboleiros (people tasked with pulling the ropes) will swing it across the crowds at great speed, emitting strong bursts of incense.

Because Santiago is the terminus of the Camino, it is a very busy city. There's plenty to see and do and it contains a wide array of cafés and restaurants for weary pilgrims.

Virginie and I were on the road by seven. The first 15 minutes of our walk took us on a loop that brought us back almost to the front door of our hostel. We hadn't realized, through our fatigue, how close we actually were to getting back on the trail. It added an extra 15 minutes of walking but on the last day of this epic journey, it only generated a laugh from both of us. An hour later, we stopped into a café for breakfast. We both agreed that the warm chocolate croissant was easily the best of the entire trip.

The trail was absolutely packed with walkers to the point of aggravation. It was slow going. It wasn't that we were in a particular hurry, but it all seemed a bit jarring after hundreds of kilometres of relative solitude.

I'm sure it was the adrenaline of knowing that the final destination awaited us in a few hours, but I felt very strong in the home stretch. Of course, all of this walking had gotten me in pretty good physical shape.

We stopped about five kilometres outside our endpoint, and it was a three-ring circus. Because so many pilgrims time their final day to arrive in Santiago at lunchtime, this locale was teeming with people. We stopped for refreshments and had to stand in line for food and bathrooms.

Santiago stretched out in front of us as we stood on a hill high above the city. It didn't seem possible that this was the end of the line. Getting from the outskirts into the core of the city takes a considerable amount of time. Most pilgrims head directly for the Catedral de Santiago de Compostela and the grand plaza to officially end their Camino. Every major city along the route has a plaza or square, usually situated near the main cathedral. There are typically shops and restaurants all around the outer edges of the plaza. We decided to go to our albergue and get cleaned up first. The Seminario Menor is one of the most traditional accommodations for pilgrims in Santiago, offering a great view of the city. As the name suggests, this was once a seminary. It is a massive structure and harkens back to a time when many young men regarded the religious life as a calling.

Most albergues will not allow pilgrims to stay multiple nights, but that was not the case here. We both planned to stay one extra day and elected for a two-night reservation. I inquired about a private room and there were plenty available. The cost of a room with bunkbeds was 10 Euros; the private room was 17 Euros. My room was austere but perfect, with a communal bathroom directly across the hall.

After a mandatory shower, we headed toward the Catedral. Although there was one street musician–a lone bagpiper, playing near the entrance to the great plaza beside the church–there was no other fanfare. There were hundreds of pilgrims embracing one another and group photography was the order of the day. It felt a bit odd and definitely anticlimactic. It may be trite to say, but the Camino is truly about the journey and not the destination–except, perhaps, for true religious pilgrims.

We entered the Catedral but unfortunately it was undergoing repairs at the time and we were unable to see very much. This also removed any possibility of seeing the giant Botafumeiro the next day at the pilgrim mass at noon.

For most walkers, getting the cherished Compostela certificate is the culmination of the walk. We wandered down to the official Pilgrim Office, and the lineup stretched to Portugal. We were told that the wait could be up to two hours, and we opted to come back the next day. Food and drink were much higher priorities than a piece of parchment. We made our way to a sundrenched outdoor café and toasted each other.

Having promised my friend Rami that I would get a tattoo upon completion of the Camino, Virginie and I took a stroll to Old Skull Tattoo and Piercing. The name seemed more than appropriate for me. It just needed the word "bald" in front of skull. I had heard that this was the premiere shop in Santiago. Even using Google Maps, the location of the shop was elusive. We entered and were met by two people, the receptionist and the artist. The place was clean and the people were very friendly. I showed them the hand drawn concept piece from Aleksandra and they assured me that they could reproduce it without any difficulty. I booked an appointment for the following day and put down a deposit of 40 Euros.

I was quite pumped leaving the shop. We hadn't walked far when Virginie said that she didn't like the feel of the place. I always—well, most of the time—opt for a woman's intuition. I decided to sleep on it before making a final decision.

We went back to our albergue, where I was able to do laundry. The laundry facility was in the basement of this massive building. There was also a huge cafeteria near the laundry, as well as a kitchen where pilgrims could cook their own meals. Mercifully, I was the only one doing laundry and didn't have to face the usual frenzy to get washers and dryers. I wrote in my journal while I did my laundry, all the while watching pilgrims from many countries prepare their dinner in the kitchen. The smells were divine.

After a short nap, Virginie and I headed back to the plaza. A number of stages were being erected in preparation for a three-day festival due to start the following day. The city was packed with pilgrims and tourists. Santiago must have one of the largest concentrations of bars and restaurants on the planet. We walked the streets for some time, trying to find the best spot to eat. One in particular was packed and had a sizeable lineup but we could tell there was something special about this place.

A Taberna de Bispo is a "must go" place in Santiago. Because there were just two of us, we didn't have to wait long and scored a seat at a lengthy counter. The food was spectacular. The tapas bar seemed to go on forever and the choices of food were mind numbing. We sampled many of them, along with some excellent red wine. It was only well into the meal that I realized that this was the exact restaurant recommended by my family member who'd done the Camino last year!

We meandered through the streets of the city on that warm Galician night, not saying a whole lot, trying to process the events of the previous 25 days.

Pamplona to Santiago de Compostela: 713 kilometres and 1,023,293 steps.

Camino Tip # 25: Don't Expect a Welcome Party at the End of the Camino

Contrary to what one might expect after such an epic journey, the Camino ends abruptly and without fanfare. Beyond the people who happen to be walking with you on your final day, there isn't an official welcoming committee in the great plaza–unless you count the bagpiper!

Chapter 26 – Santiago de Compostela

Just like that, it was all over.

Twenty-five days and over 700 kilometres later, my Camino had come to an end. The feeling was similar to completing the Boston Marathon. While there was a sense of satisfaction and a hint of joy, it was mostly relief. Of course, there is also some sadness knowing that the real world lurks just around the corner, as everyone must go back to their home countries.

Having witnessed the massive lineups at the Pilgrim Office the previous day, I headed there bright and early on my last day. The office opens at eight o'clock in the morning and when I arrived at a quarter past seven, there was already a short lineup waiting to get in. I decided to grab a quick breakfast at a café a few doors down. By the time I returned the lineup had doubled, as dozens of people were streaming through the streets to get their Compostela certificate.

I noticed at least one familiar face in the crowd, the ubiquitous Lily from Russia! She was one of the first people to exit the Pilgrim Office clutching her certificate. My wait was reasonably short at 45 minutes and I, too, could now officially call myself a pilgrim.

My plan for the day was quite simple. I knew that several of my friends would be arriving today, so I would spend much of my time hanging around the plaza. However, the first order of business was to go back to Old Skull Tattoo and Piercing to cancel my appointment and see if I could have my deposit returned. I had given it a lot of thought last night and decided it would be more prudent to have the tattoo done back in my hometown by someone with an established reputation. Besides, with more travel days in front of me, I didn't want to risk infection by not being able to treat the new tattoo properly. I received my refund, but my resolve to get a tattoo had not diminished.

By mid-morning, many familiar faces had streamed into the great plaza. Knowing that most people would be attending the pilgrims' mass, this was the best time to welcome fellow walkers. I exchanged hugs and well wishes with Karen (Sweden), Hans (Netherlands), Klaus (Germany) and Jin (South Korea). There were lots of high fives and selfies and exuberance filled the air.

Virginie showed up in the plaza after getting her Compostela certificate and we decided to attend the mass at noon. The church was packed with some 2,000 pilgrims. The mass was in Spanish and it was very warm indoors. Not being able to understand a word and having been relegated to standing at the very back of the church, we both bailed partway through.

I met up with Felicity and we had lunch together at a café beside the cathedral. She was one of my favourite people I'd met on the Camino. She has faced a lot of adversity in her young life, yet she sparkles with enthusiasm.

While hanging around the plaza in the afternoon, I was approached by half a dozen students. They looked to be young teenagers and hey were working on a school project, interviewing people who had just completed their Camino. They were delightful and I was greeted with shrieks of joy when I gave each of them a small pin of the Canada flag.

Late in the afternoon, I met up with Aleksandra, Magdalena and four of their walking friends: Antonio, Paula, Nicolas and Javi. They had just received their Compostela certificate and were going to a bar to celebrate. The name of the bar was Canadu. We drank wine and toasted each other. While we were eating, Nicolas was busy across the table sketching. As we were about to clink glasses for the umpteenth time, he presented a drawing, which represented the traditional Spanish toast containing the words *arriba, abajo, al centro, y para dentro*. Arriba is the signal to raise your glass towards the heavens; abajo means to bring the glass back down; al centro means to bring your glass to the center and y para dentro means inside, where the wine belongs!

Aleksandra and Magdalena had to catch a bus for Portugal, so I decided to walk there with them and purchase my own ticket, as I planned to travel to Porto the next day. It was a frantic walk as they were running behind. We arrived mere moments before the bus left the terminal.

Once I'd seen my friends off and secured my ticket, I returned to the Catedral. On the side opposite the great plaza is another smaller plaza, the epicentre for the concerts of the three-day festival. A big evening of music was about to get underway. I met Jin and two of her walking companions, Jesus and Allefair. We didn't have much of an opportunity to chat, as the concert began with some very loud warm-up acts.

I handed out the last of my Canadian pins. Jin put one in her ear while the waiter and bartender put them on their shirts.

The crowd seemed to multiply by the minute as the evening wore on, and long before the main act was to take the stage there were thousands of people jammed into the square. I was getting tired and after three hours of increasingly cramped quarters, I decided to duck out. I pushed and shoved my way through the throng. The streets of the city were also packed with revellers. It seemed like everyone in Santiago was in a party mood.

I left the hubbub of the downtown core and made my way back to Semanario Menor. I stood on the steps of the old seminary, looking back on the city somewhat wistfully.

Antonio de la Sotilla

Sixty-six year old Antonio lives in Barcelona, Spain. He had a successful business career. He was the general manager of one of the biggest ski resorts in Europe after managing a large financial company. For 20 years, he owned and operated an industrial maintenance company, which he sold three years ago. He's sailed across the Atlantic twice and the Mediterranean Sea on three occasions. To celebrate his fiftieth birthday he decided to do a few stages of the Camino, and since that time he's covered the Camino Francés, the Camino from Oporto and the Camino from Le Pui in France, typically with family members and friends.

This Camino holds special meaning for Antonio. A few months ago, his nephew, a motorcycle racer, was involved in a terrible accident that left him a paraplegic. Antonio visited him several times in the hospital and his nephew gave him a rosary to carry along the Camino to Santiago. Antonio feels confident that he may someday walk the Camino with his nephew by his side.

"The Camino has a unique ambience. It gives me time alone with my thoughts. By the time I reach Santiago de Compostela, I have forged new relationships. I start the journey alone but always finish it with friends."

Paula Alejandra Martinez

Paula was born in Argentina. She is a public accountant and works as an administrator in the Ministry of Education in Córdoba.

For her first trip to Europe she decided to walk the Camino primarily as a personal challenge. "I wanted to be able to face things on my own, using my own skills and resources. I knew that this was going to be an amazing experience."

According to Paula, the walk was magical. Every day and every kilometre seemed to provide something new and different. "Each day, I got up and left the albergue, never quite knowing what to expect. I came in contact with wonderful people from all over the world. They quickly became my road family."

She describes the experience as unrepeatable and unique. "The road was fabulous. From the beginning, I surrendered to the trail and let things unfold. What captured my heart were the people. You never felt alone on the Camino. I was able to share my day with my new friends."

Jesus Sanchis

Jesus is from Valencia, Spain, the third largest city in the country nestled along the shores of the Mediterranean Sea. He is a journalist working at the EFE News Agency, a public international company providing news from all over the world. He is currently based in Madrid.

143

Over the years, Jesus had heard a lot about the Camino. Friends had told him about their experiences on the walk where they tried to find the answers to some questions about their lives. "I was looking for something like that. I wanted to take some days just for me, to disconnect from work, bills, problems, even from my family and friends! You know, sometimes you just want to be alone for a while."

While Jesus didn't find answers to the big questions of life, he found other things which were every bit as valuable. "The most important thing I learned was letting go of things or simply going with the flow.

The connection with other walkers was very important too. "When you walk alone over some hours and the only sounds you hear are your own footsteps, the wind, and the birds, it is very comforting to meet up with people to share your experiences, which enriches your own trip."

He also enjoyed the beautiful landscapes, the delicious Spanish food and the physical exertion. It also gave Jesus an opportunity to hone his English language skills, as more than 60% of the people he met along the way weren't Spanish-speaking.

"I am proud of my country and so happy to receive so many visitors from every part of the world."

Javier Pando

144

Javier was born in Madrid, Spain and now lives in Cambrils, a coastal town in the province of Tarragona, Catalonia, Spain. He is a technical architect and worked in the real estate department of an insurance company. Although not officially retired, he is rapidly approaching that day.

Javier decided to do the Camino at the urging of his friend, Antonio.

The Camino experience has left a lasting impression upon Javier. "I found the long walk across Spain has enriched my life. It had a very positive impact on me."

Upon reflection, three keys themes emerged for Javier:

1. Respect. Javier discovered that people walking the Camino respect fellow walkers

2. Equality. Everyone on the Camino is different. They come from different walks of life, different socioeconomic status and from different parts of the world. "On the Camino, we are all equals."

3. Friendship. Javier met many new people and forged friendships that he'll treasure for a long time.

Camino Tip #26: Cherish Your Camino Friends

Even when you're physically by yourself, you're never really alone on the Camino. You meet the most amazing, kind and generous people from all over the world while walking the trail. Be thankful that they were with you when you needed them most. Revel in the conversations you had, and the laughter and tears you shared on this remarkable journey.

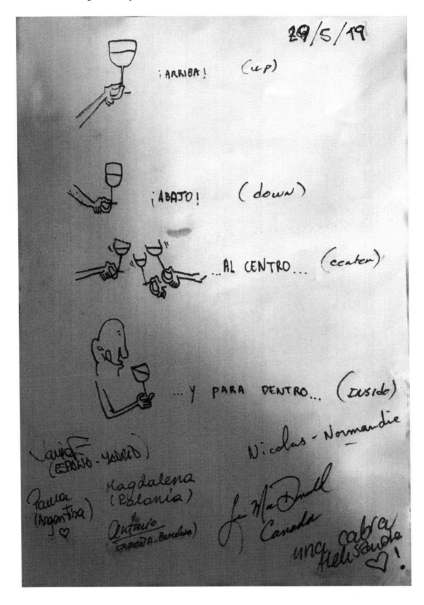

Epilogue

PORTUGAL

On May 30th, what would have been my late mother's 94th birthday, I walked through the streets of Santiago for the last time as I made my way up the steep hills to the bus station. I dozed and read a bit on the four-hour trip to Portugal.

When I got off the bus in Porto, it felt like a steam bath. It was 35 degrees and the humidity was stifling. I had arranged to meet my two Polish friends at the main bus station, but somehow our wires had gotten crossed. They'd wound up at the other station in Porto, some seven kilometres from the city centre. I found a small, non-air-conditioned café a short walk from the bus terminal. I was drenched in sweat.

I had a fantastic lunch, the house special, which consisted of pataniscous de bacalhau (salt codfish cakes) with rice, veggie and hot sausage, along with the now requisite cold beer. I discovered two Canadian pins in my pocket, which I handed out to the wait staff.

I had several hours to kill before taking possession of my Airbnb, so I spent the afternoon walking the streets of Porto. The place was absolutely packed with tourists and locals alike, and the streets were just humming with activity. I thought Santiago had a lot of bars and cafés, but that city paled in comparison to Porto.

I found a bank machine, withdrew some cash and had an ice cream to cool me down. I even checked out a tattoo parlour just to kill some time.

I checked in to my Airbnb around dinnertime. There were three rooms: two in the front overlooking a busy street, and one at the rear, which turned out to be mine. For a moment I thought I had hit pay dirt, not having to listen to traffic. I was mistaken. My bedroom looked out upon a neighborhood that couldn't be seen from the main streets. It was a collection of small homes and every single one of them was a miniature farm, complete with animals. The one directly below my window happened to have a rooster. I wasn't overly concerned, having once owned a rooster myself, but I was soon to discover that this particular bird never shut up. He crowed morning, noon and night.

I met one of my roommates, Moailton Mesquita Lopes Filho, a young civil lawyer from Brazil. Travelling is his hobby and his passion. He had been in Porto for several days and was planning to travel to England, Ireland and Italy before returning home. I invited him to spend the evening with me, Aleksandra and Magdalena.

We met up with the others and headed in to the heart of the city. We were ravenous and decided to get some food before a night of revelling.

I casually asked a waiter at one of what felt like 10,000 sidewalk cafés what one might eat that best represented Portugal. He pointed to something on the menu. It was in Portugese, but I am nothing if not adventurous and I gave him the two thumbs up. I was about to experience Francesinha for the very first time.

Do you remember the "Double Down" sandwich that KFC was offering several years ago? You know, the one where two deep fried chicken breasts replace the normal bun that one would find in a fast food restaurant? Wedged inside this were bacon, cheese and the Colonel's special sauce. I did exhaustive research on Wikipedia (!) and was astonished to learn that this delicacy tips the scale at a modest five hundred and forty calories. *Really?* I'm thinking that a

Senate investigation might be in order to confirm the veracity of this claim.

The warm evening and the glow of Port had me feeling quite mellow. That is, until the Francesinha was presented in all of its heart-stopping glory. And what, pray tell, are the ingredients in this artery-clogging masterpiece?

I'll start with a few of the more benign. There's some cornstarch to thicken the gravy, tomato paste and a harmless bay leaf. There's milk, chili flakes and salt. Now is where things take a serious turn toward the emergency room. The other main ingredients of a Francesinha are bread (thankfully not two deep fried chicken breasts), roast beef, chorizo, smoked ham, Dutch cheese, beer and Port. Sitting atop this eighth wonder of the modern world is a fried egg. The sandwich is served with enough French fries to satisfy the palates of an entire class of kindergarten children.

I must admit that all 1,300 calories (not including the fries) were very tasty, but the mutiny I imagined was being staged by my arteries took some of the fun out of tackling this monster. I reckoned that the strain on my heart might be akin to attaching chains to my back and trying to pull a bus for 100 metres.

We dragged ourselves down to the Duoro River, which was teeming with people. Aleksandra and Magdalena had hatched a plan earlier in the day and while we sat on the quay they produced a bottle of Port, along with some plastic glasses, procured at a bar on our way to the river. We toasted each other and looked across the river at the city of Vila Nova de Gaia, the hub of the Port industry in Portugal. Every major winery has a facility in this city and their signs light up the night sky.

A second bottle was produced, and the party ended in the wee hours of the morning. Two and a half hours later, my loud, feathered friend announced the arrival of a new day.

Slightly bedraggled, I headed to the train station around eight o'clock in the morning to procure a ticket for Madrid. The friendly ticket agent gave me lots of helpful information and advised me that the first leg of my trip would take me to the city of Coimbra, where I would spend the day before catching an overnight train to Madrid.

I reconnected with my friends from the previous night to spend a final day in Porto. We had planned to go to the beach but with very heavy traffic, we decided that it wasn't worth the effort, especially with the women needing to catch an afternoon flight back home. We spent more time on the waterfront before bidding one another farewell. In the evening, Moailton and I walked across the bridge to Vila Nova de Gaia and had a great pizza as the sun set over the Douro.

The following morning, Moailton walked me to the train station. He knew a woman from Brazil who was doing a Master's program at the University of Coimbra. He called her and made arrangements for me to drop off my knapsack at her apartment while I spent the day wandering.

I enjoyed the day in Coimbra and spent 10 Euros to be able to tour a famous library at the university, which was established in 1920 and steeped in history. Some of the books are so old and rare that they're kept in special rooms, rather than on display. Bats can be seen flying around the library to eat moths that can otherwise destroy these invaluable books. Getting to and from the university is a physical challenge, as Coimbra has some extremely steep hills.

SPAIN

I had decided to go back to Pamplona to visit Andrea Jiminez. She is a young opera singer whom I met on the train from Madrid to Pamplona when I'd first arrived in Spain a month earlier.

The overnight train to Madrid didn't have any sleeping cars available, so I had to sit up for the entire ride.

Having been in the Atocha railway station in Madrid earlier in the trip, I knew what to expect. What I didn't anticipate was the aftermath of the UEFA Champions League soccer final the previous evening. The train station was mayhem as thousands of inebriated soccer fans swarmed the facility. The Atocha station has obviously seen this type of behaviour after previous major football events, and there was extra security and police presence. It was a rather pathetic scene but the trains still ran like clockwork, leaving many latecomers dazed and confused when they missed their trains.

I arrived in Pamplona in the late afternoon and walked to Hotel Yoldi, where I had stayed the night prior to beginning the Camino. On my way, I passed the exact spot where I had started my walk and looked wistfully at three pilgrims heading down the trail. I spent the evening in the plaza, watching flamenco dancers while sipping wine and doing laundry.

I met up with Andrea the next morning for breakfast. Afterwards, she took me to a piano recital at the Pamplona Conservatory of Music. The pianist was a professional from another country, but in order to be able to perform here he'd come to the Conservatory two years ago to obtain his Spanish credentials. The concert was exquisite and the acoustics in the performance hall were magnificent. When he finished a piece and lifted his fingers from the keys, the notes hung in the air like a hummingbird at a feeder. It had been a wonderful day. Pamplona is a great city and I vowed to someday come back and witness the running of the bulls.

FRANCE

I took an afternoon bus to Biarritz, France. On the bus, I met two women from Dublin, Ireland, who had just completed the last leg of the Camino from Sarria. I told them that my ancestors came from Tralee. They smiled and said, "Oh, you mean The Kingdom." So religious are the folks in this county Kerry city that they have their own designation!

Biarritz, located in southwest France near the Spanish border, is a tourist city and a major stopping off point for pilgrims planning to do the Camino. Walkers from around the world generally fly to Paris and take a second flight to Biarritz, followed by a bus or train trip to Saint-Jean-Pied-de-Port, which is the beginning of the Camino Francés.

My Airbnb, arranged by my friend Jan, was no more than 200 metres from the ocean. It was conveniently located in a facility that housed a cool bar. I dined on raw tuna, wasabi and, of course, French wine. The beach was spectacular.

For some strange reason, I hadn't been able to check in online for my noon flight from Biarritz to Paris. I'd decided to go to the airport early in the morning and take care of this, but discovered that the check-in counter wouldn't open until an hour before the flight.

I spent the next few hours wandering the coastline of Biarritz. It is obviously a surfer's paradise. I headed back to the airport and got in line to get my boarding pass. When I reached the counter of Easyjet, I was informed that the flight was full (overbooked) and because I hadn't checked in online, I was now considered a standby passenger. Normally this would have caused me some consternation but I reckoned that if I couldn't get on this flight, I could go back into Biarritz and lounge on the beach for the afternoon, as the next flight wasn't until midnight. I was told to come back at noon, 15 minutes before the flight was scheduled to leave.

As I awaited my fate, I did what any intrepid traveler would do: I went to an airport café, ordered a flan and a café au lait, and started working on my Plan B.

At noon, I approached the check-in counter for the second time that day. The clerk issued my boarding pass and personally escorted me through a private security check, getting me to my gate in time to board the plane. There were a number of empty seats on the flight, and I sat in a row by myself. Go figure.

I arrived at the Charles de Gaulle Airport and took a train into Paris where I met my niece, Shelley, at an outdoor café. I spent a very pleasant evening with Shelley and her husband André, who had done the Camino several years ago. Shelley prepared a mouth-watering supper and I was very happy to sleep on their couch. The nearest hotel was asking 300 Euros.

I was on the go early the next morning and headed off on foot to see Notre-Dame de Paris Cathedral, a Paris landmark devastated by fire in April 2019. I walked along the Seine River to the cathedral but there wasn't much to see, as it was barricaded and surrounded by armed guards. I got on the Métro and headed to Montmartre where I would rendezvous with Janneke, a friend from the Netherlands whom I'd met during my time in southern India a few years ago.

By the time we met up, it had turned into a rainy and cold evening; it was far too messy to do any walking, so we went to a restaurant nearby and had the largest hamburgers either of us had ever seen before heading to our Airbnb.

Near the end of the 19th century and the beginning of the 20th, many artists lived or worked in or around Montmartre, including Monet, Renoir, Degas, Picasso and van Gogh. According to the owner of the Airbnb, a good friend of Piccaso had occupied this very suite.

We spent the following day walking through Paris. With very limited time, we decided to avoid the major landmarks, as it would have required a lot of time on trains. We spent most of the day in Montmartre visiting a famous graveyard, passing the Moulin Rouge and walking down to the Louvre Museum.

The following morning, I headed to the airport to catch my flight back to Canada.

Adieu, France. Adios, Spain. Tchau, Portugal.